Build and Sail Your Own Boat

Norman Dahl

Build and Sail
Your Own Boat

Based on the Ulster Television Series

Stanley Paul, London

Stanley Paul & Co Ltd
3 Fitzroy Square, London W1P 6JD

An imprint of the Hutchinson Publishing Group

London Melbourne Sydney Auckland
Wellington Johannesburg and agencies
throughout the world

First published 1978
© IDTV Enterprises Ltd 1978

Set in Monotype Times

Printed in Great Britain at The Anchor Press Ltd
and bound by Wm Brendon & Son Ltd
both of Tiptree, Essex

ISBN 0 09 132770 9 (cased)
ISBN 0 09 132771 7 (paper)

Contents

Acknowledgements

The author would like to acknowledge the technical assistance given by the following in the preparation of this book:

Jack Holt Limited
Strand Glassfibre Limited
Timber Research and Development Association
Ciba-Geigy Plastics and Additives Company

Introduction

The popularity of small boats never seems to stop growing. At weekends and on summer evenings, more and more people make their way to some stretch of water, a dinghy on the roof of their car, or on a trailer behind it. Once on the water, they can do whatever they please – race under sail, potter about in creeks and backwaters, go fishing, or do anything else that takes their fancy. Even in an age of rising prices, messing about in a small boat need not be expensive. A dinghy need cost no more than a modest hi-fi system, and can give as much pleasure for just as long. The introduction of modern materials, in particular plywood, glues and glass-fibre resins, has led to the introduction of a number of attractive and enjoyable dinghies which can be made up from kits. Such boats are both easy to build and reasonably priced.

This book is primarily intended for people who want to join in this expanding activity and build a boat for themselves and their family. They may know something about boats, but are apprehensive about the difficulty of building one; or perhaps they are already home handymen who would like to try their hand at building a boat, but who do not know how to use it once it has been built. This book will serve its purpose if it reassures both these kinds of people that it is easy, enjoyable and very satisfying to build and sail your own boat.

1 The Ideal Boat

The first step in deciding which dinghy you want to build, out of the profusion of designs available, is to be quite clear what you want your boat to do. If you wish to race, then you want a Class boat, preferably one that is raced by a club nearby that you can join. If you want to take the family out, then the boat must be big and stable enough to carry them safely. If you want to teach the kids to sail, then the boat must be responsive, forgiving and easy for them to manage. A fisherman wants a stable, seaworthy platform with plenty of room for people, gear and (hopefully) fish.

Almost every prospective boat owner will draw up a different list of the qualities he wants in his boat. The next difficulty is to know how well any particular boat among the many on the market will meet his requirements. One way, not very effective, is to ask the advice of more knowledgeable friends, but the only really effective way to get to know about boats is to own and use one yourself. For the complete newcomer, the safest course is to choose a boat designed to do many things – to be an all-purpose boat. In fact, it is impossible to design a boat that is truly all-purpose. Every design of boat is a series of compromises between mutually exclusive requirements. So, while a so-called all-purpose boat is unlikely to be outstandingly good in any one task, it can, if well designed, be quite respectably good in a number of different jobs.

This book is concerned largely with the Ideal dinghy, which is just such an all-purpose boat (*Figure 1*). It was designed by one of the world's leading dinghy designers, Jack Holt, who has been responsible for some of the most successful dinghies ever built, both in terms of numbers and performance. Over 150000 Jack-Holt-designed boats have been built, in a variety of classes that includes such well-known names as the GP14, the Enterprise and the Mirror.

The Ideal dinghy is Jack Holt's conception, after a lifetime's experience, of the perfect family boat. It is 12 ft 3 in. (3·7 m) long,

Plate 1: The Ideal dinghy.

Figure 1: The Ideal dinghy.

Plate 2: Jack Holt, designer of the Ideal.

with a beam of 5 ft 3 in. (1·6 m). It can carry four adults in comfort, and is remarkably stable. It is sturdily built, but at the same time is light enough for two people to lift without effort. It can be propelled by oars or outboard motor, and has a simple, seaman-like rig that gives a crisp and exhilarating performance under sail. At the same time, her stability means that she can be safely and easily managed by children. The thought given to the design even extends to the provision of a waterproof stowage for dry clothes, valuables and supplies both solid and liquid. As well as this, the Ideal has been designed to be easy to build from a kit by anyone with only a modest knowledge of using woodworking tools.

While this book is based on the Ideal dinghy, it is not essential to buy an Ideal to get value from it. The basic constructional techniques described apply to a number of other types of dinghy. The assembly instructions will differ in detail only. And the chapters on using a boat apply equally well to any dinghy of about the same size.

One decision that has to be made very early on is whether to build your boat from a kit of parts or from a set of drawings. For the first-time builder, a kit is by far the better proposition. A kit is complete, with all the parts cut to the correct shape from the right materials, and with a set of detailed instructions. A kit is also likely to be cheaper; because the kit manufacturer can buy and machine his timber in bulk, it will probably cost less than the same timber from your local timber merchant, assuming that he stocks the proper types of wood for boat-building. But if you have set your heart on a type of dinghy that is not available in kit form, then you have no choice but to go it alone. In this book you will find advice on the selection of timber, and some of the boat-building techniques you will need.

Once you have built your boat, and she lies gleaming in her new paint, you will want to rush off to the water and take her out. At this moment, you may feel the need for some support. Sailors come in many sorts; some are solitary, seeking no company but their own. Others are madly gregarious, and sail round buoys in tight little packs. For the newcomer to small boats, a course somewhere in the middle is probably best. The hurly-burly of racing takes some getting used to, but there is much comfort and wisdom to be drawn from the company of other sailors. Try to join a yacht club in the area in which you want to sail. If you do not know what clubs there are, the Royal Yachting Association, Victoria Way, Woking, Surrey will be able to tell you. The RYA also organizes training schemes for budding sailors, and can tell you about them as well. An RYA-approved school offers a high standard of instruction, but can be rather expensive. If you have children who want to learn to sail, your local Education Authority may well run a sailing school to which they could go.

2 Nautical Names

The newcomer to boats and sailing is often baffled by the strange language that sailors use, full of unfamiliar words. Even ordinary words seem to take on an entirely different meaning. Some people think this is mere affectation, and they resolutely stick to everyday English – front and back rather than bow and stern, or left and right instead of port and starboard. But it is sensible and satisfying to use the correct terms in building and sailing a boat, because these words have evolved over the centuries to describe clearly and precisely what boat-builders and seamen wish to say. Take for example the word 'beating'. This is the term used to describe the way in which a sailing boat is handled so as to make progress against the wind. After you have studied Chapter 10, you will appreciate that this is not difficult to do, but that the explanation is quite involved. Once you understand the process, the advantage of having a short and simple word to describe it will be obvious.

This chapter is in three parts: *Figure 2* names the parts of a boat, and *Figure 3* names the various bits and pieces used in sailing. The glossary defines other terms commonly used in sailing. You may find it better to glance through the chapter at the first reading, and to refer back to it as unfamiliar words appear later in the book. Use the proper terms whenever you can, even when just thinking about the subject, and they will soon become second nature.

Glossary

AFT	Towards the stern, but inside the boat.
ABACK	A sail is aback when its clew is held to windward (Chapter 10).
ABEAM	Away to one side of the boat, at right angles to the fore and aft line.
ABAFT	Towards the stern, but outside the boat. An object may be described as being 'abaft the beam'.

ASTERN	Behind the boat.
BACK	1 To sheet the clew of a sail to windward so it is set aback. The jib can be backed to make the boat pay off in the right direction (Chapter 10). 2 The wind is said to back when its direction changes anti-clockwise (e.g. from north to west).
BEAM	The greatest width of the boat.
BEAR AWAY	To turn the boat away from the direction of the wind.
BEATING	The process of handling a boat so that it makes progress against the wind (Chapter 10).
BEND ON	To fasten a rope or a sail to a spar.
BLOCK	An enclosed pulley used to change the lead, or direction, of a rope.
BOW	The front part of a boat.
BULKHEAD	An upright partition across the width of the boat.
BY THE LEE	When the wind comes over the same side of the boat as the boom. It can occur when running and should be avoided, as it may lead to an inadvertent gybe (Chapter 10).
CAST OFF	To let go of mooring lines and proceed.
CLEAT	A fitting to which a rope can be made fast.
CLOSE HAULED	Sailing as close to the wind as possible.
COAMING	A piece of wood round the edge of a deck which stops any water on the deck from running into the boat.
EASE SHEETS	To let out the sheets, adjusting the set of the sail.
EYE OF THE WIND	The direction from which the wind is blowing.
FAIRLEAD	A fitting for changing the lead, or direction of a rope. Unlike a block, it has no moving parts.
FORWARD	Towards the bow. It is pronounced 'forrard'.
GAFF	A spar which extends the top of a sail above the masthead.
GOING ABOUT	Turning the bow of the boat through the eye of the wind from one tack to the other. Also called 'tacking'.
GOOSE WINGED	When the mainsail and the jib are set on opposite sides of the boat while running.
GUDGEON AND PINTLE	The fittings that hold the rudder onto the stern. Pintles are the pins on the rudder, and

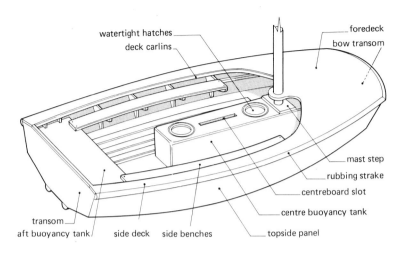

watertight hatches
deck carlins
foredeck
bow transom
mast step
rubbing strake
centreboard slot
centre buoyancy tank
transom
aft buoyancy tank
side deck
side benches
topside panel

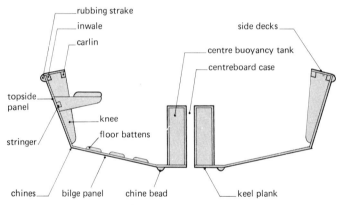

rubbing strake
inwale
carlin
side decks
centre buoyancy tank
centreboard case
topside panel
knee
floor battens
stringer
chines
bilge panel
chine bead
keel plank

Figure 2: The parts of a boat.

gudgeons are the rings on the transom into which the pintles fit.

GYBING Turning the stern of the boat through the eye of the wind. It is the opposite of going about.

HARDEN SHEETS To pull the sheets in to adjust the set of the sail.

HEAVE TO To use the sails and rudder to make the boat lie comfortably stopped in the water.

HELM Another name for the tiller, which is the lever that turns the rudder.

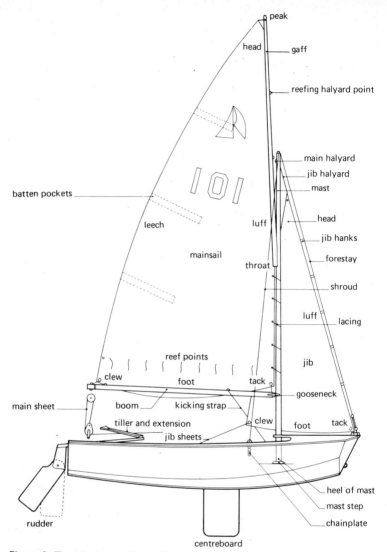

peak

head

gaff

reefing halyard point

main halyard

jib halyard

mast

head

batten pockets

jib hanks

luff

forestay

leech

shroud

mainsail

luff

lacing

throat

jib

reef points

clew

foot

tack

gooseneck

main sheet

boom

kicking strap

clew

foot

tack

tiller and extension

jib sheets

heel of mast

mast step

rudder

chainplate

centreboard

Figure 3: The Ideal rigged for sailing.

HOG

A piece of wood which runs along the bottom of the boat from bow to stern. The hog is fitted inside the skin of the boat, as opposed to the keel, which is fitted outside. Many modern dinghies do not have a hog or a keel.

IN IRONS

A boat is in irons when it is lying head to wind with no steerage way, and therefore cannot manoeuvre.

Plate 3: The Ideal dinghy rigged for sailing.

KNEE	A piece of wood, roughly triangular in shape, which holds two parts fixed at right angles to each other.
LEE	The side of an object away from the wind.
LEE SHORE	A shore with the wind blowing on it from seaward.
LEEWARD	Towards the lee side. It is pronounced 'loo-ard'.

LUFF	1 The leading edge of a sail.
	2 To turn a boat so that it points closer to the wind.
MAKE FAST	To fasten a rope securely.
MAST STEP	The socket into which the heel, or bottom, of the mast fits.
PAINTER	The mooring line by which a boat is made fast to a buoy or jetty.
PAY OFF	A boat pays off when its bow is blown downwind.
PINCHING	When close hauled, sailing the boat closer to the wind than it will efficiently go.
PORT	The left hand side of the boat, looking forward.
PULLING	Another word for rowing.
QUARTER	The side of a boat between the beam and the stern.
REACH	Any point of sailing between close hauled and running. A close reach means that the wind is before the beam; a beam reach means that the wind is on the beam; and a broad reach means that the wind is abaft the beam.
REEF	To reduce the area of a sail.
REEF POINTS	Short lengths of line sewn to some sails, to gather up the part of the sail not used when it has been reefed.
ROWLOCKS	Swivelling brackets for oars.
RUBBING STRAKE	A piece of wood or rubber fixed to the gunwhale of a boat to protect it against damage.
RUNNING	A boat is running when the wind is coming over the stern.
SHEET	A rope fixed to the clew of a sail to control it.
SHIP	To fit something in place.
SPAR	A rigid support for the edge of a sail. The gaff and the boom are spars, but the mast is not.
STARBOARD	The right side of the boat, looking forward.
STERN	The back part of the boat.
TACKING	*See* 'Going about'.
THWART	A seat running across the boat. Pronounced 'thort'.
TRIM	1 The attitude of a boat in the water. A boat may be trimmed by the head, trimmed by the stern, or have a list to port or starboard.
	2 To adjust the trim of a boat, by moving weights about (in a dinghy, usually the crew).

3 To trim a sail is to adjust the sheet so that the sail sets properly.

UNSHIP   To remove something from its proper place.

VEER   The wind is said to veer when its direction changes clockwise.

WARP   A strong piece of rope used for towing or anchoring.

WAY   A boat is making way when it is moving through the water.

WEATHER   The side of an object onto which the wind is blowing.

WEATHER SHORE   A shore where the wind is blowing from the land towards the sea.

YAW   Uncontrolled variations in a boat's course, caused by wind and sea conditions.

3 Wood for Boats

Wood is by far the most suitable material for the amateur to use in building a boat. It is easy to get, easy to work and repair, it takes glues and other fastenings well, it is inherently buoyant and it looks good. A beginner can best buy his wood as a kit, in which all the parts are already cut to shape, of the correct material, and reasonably cheap. However, if you cannot find a kit boat that meets your needs and decide to build a boat from plans, then you will have to choose and buy your own wood. Provided you know what you are looking for, this is no real problem, and you should get a lot of help from the cutting list supplied with the plans of your chosen boat. The biggest difficulty will probably lie in finding a timber merchant who stocks the high-quality timber and marine plywood that you will need.

Plywood

Almost every small craft is nowadays built of plywood, because of the many advantages that this material offers. Plywood construction is much simpler than the old methods of planking a boat. It is a consistent material, whereas good-quality solid timber is expensive and hard to find. And plywood is stronger; a ply skin on a boat is about twice as strong as solid planking of the same thickness, leading to savings both in weight and cost.

Plywood is made by peeling logs of suitable timber to produce thin sheets of veneer. Several layers of veneer are then bonded together under heat and pressure to produce the ply. The most widely used plywood in small-boat construction has three plies; the grains of the two outside plies run in the same direction, and the core ply grain runs at right angles to them. There can be more than three plies, and many different kinds of plywood are made, all with different properties. For example, it is possible to make a multi-plywood which is much stiffer in one direction than in the other; such a ply is used for centreboards, which must resist a sideways bending load.

There are three factors which determine the quality of a plywood and hence its suitability for use in boat-building. They are:

The natural durability of the wood

The quality of the veneers

The quality of the bonding between veneers

Table 1   Timbers for marine plywoods

Common name	Natural durability	Colour
Makore	Very durable	Red
Utile	Durable	Pink
Agba (tola)	Durable	Yellow
Sapele	Moderately durable	Pink
Red serayah	Moderately durable	Pink
Khaya	Moderately durable	Red
Red keranti	Moderately durable	Pink
Gaboon	Non-durable	Pink

Table 1 describes the timbers in common use for marine plywood. They are all hardwoods, and are often loosely called 'mahogany', though strictly speaking only Khaya is genuine African Mahogany. Gaboon would appear to be the least suitable of all these woods, but it is widely used in dinghy construction because it is very much lighter than the others in the list. If the wood is properly protected by paint and varnish, the poor durability of gaboon will not affect the life of the boat to any significant extent. Boats built fifteen years ago of gaboon ply are still sailing, and are in good condition.

You can ensure that the veneers are of good quality by insisting on the highest grade of marine plywood. The only additional point to notice is that a sheet of plywood normally has a 'better' face, which has a more pleasing appearance than the other. If a piece of plywood is to be varnished, then the better face should be selected to show in the finished boat; if the plywood is to be painted, or if it is not seen in the finished boat, then the appearance of the wood is unimportant, provided the quality is still present.

For boat-building purposes, the highest standard of bonding between the plies is essential. In Britain, this quality is described as WBP, which stands for 'Water and Boil Proof'. Among the tests that a plywood has to pass before it can be graded WBP is the immersion of a sample in boiling water for seventy-two hours without delamination.

The British Standards Institute has set up a number of standards for marine plywood, of which the most important from the buyer's point of view is BS1088. For boat-building, you should ask for plywood to BS1088, with WBP adhesive. If you are using gaboon ply, then you must ask that it be supplied to BS1088 standard, as the rules are slightly different for this non-durable wood. BS4079 gives other requirements for marine plywood, and the quality of adhesives for plywood manufacture is defined in BS1203.

Because of the high pressures involved in making plywood, the size of bonding machines is limited and plywood is not generally available in sheets larger than $2\cdot4 \times 1\cdot2$ m (8×4 ft). If you require a longer piece, then you will have to join two pieces together. The thickness of plywood is quoted in millimetres, and the right thickness should be stated on the cutting list from which you are working.

Solid timber

In the construction of dinghies, mahogany can be used for almost all purposes for which ply is not. The only major exceptions are wooden masts and spars, which are made of sitka or silver spruce, western hemlock, pitch pine or larch. However, the cutting list included with the plans will specify the type of timber required for each part of the boat, as well as its size. The cutting list should be followed wherever possible, but if a particular wood is not available your timber merchant should be able to advise you of a suitable alternative. When selecting wood, examine each piece carefully, and reject any that are warped or bent (unless the piece will be bent when you fit it in the boat), and any that have irregular grain, knots, splits or sapwood. Sapwood is weaker than the rest of the tree, and it can be recognized by being lighter in colour than the bulk of the wood.

Looking after wood

When you get your wood home, whether you have bought it at a timber yard or as a kit, it needs a little care if it is to be in the best condition when you come to use it. First and foremost, it should be stored in a warm, dry place. If timber is too wet, it is difficult to glue and joints may fail in service. Wood tends to change its moisture content as the atmospheric conditions alter, and this can lead to warping; keep your wood covered up, to prevent the moisture content changing too rapidly. Mahogany tends to be a cross-grained wood, and is hence very liable to warping. Tie long lengths of mahogany with string into bundles, so that the warping tendency is cancelled out, and all the pieces remain straight.

Light can change the colour of wood, so you must prevent this happening in a way that might spoil the finished appearance of your boat. In particular, matching panels like the two sides of the foredeck should be stored with the 'better' faces together, so that they will be protected from the light, and still have the same colour when assembled.

Certain parts of the boat require very little work on them before they are installed; the side benches are one example, and the centre-board another. It is a good idea to finish off, rub down and varnish such parts at the very beginning of construction. This will protect them from moisture changes and discolouration due to light. The finished parts can be put on one side until the time comes to fit them into the boat.

4 Tools and Techniques

Tools

Although the parts in the Ideal kit arrive cut to shape, you need a few tools for assembly and final adjustment. Most of the tools required are to be found in the average handyman's toolbox. A list of recommended tools follows; some are not essential, but can save a great deal of time and effort. You will need extra tools if you are not building from a kit.

Measuring and marking

Carpenter's rule – inches and millimetres
Measuring tape – inches and millimetres, 12 ft (3·6 m) long if possible
Pencils – Carpenter's pencils are best.
A trisquare or setsquare
An adjustable bevel – only essential if building from plans
Marking gauge
Dividers
Level

Cutting tools

Tenon saw – other saws will be needed if building from scratch
Chisels – 1 in. and $\frac{1}{2}$ in. (2·5 and 1·3 cm) bevel edge
Mallet
Sharpening stone

Fixing and holding

Bench with woodworking vice – not essential for kit assembly
Screwdrivers to fit various screws; pump-action screwdriver
Hammer – Warrington No. 2 (cross pene)

Square-nosed pliers
Top cutters or side cutters
Hand drill and assortment of small bits
G cramps (2)
Pin punch

Smoothing

Plane
Surform rasp/plane

Power tools

Drill
Orbital sander
Jigsaw – if not working from a kit.

Notes

A carpenter's pencil is best for marking out; sharpen it like a chisel.

Buy good-quality tools, and look after them. Cutting tools should be kept sharp, so learn how to sharpen them before you begin.

Though a bench and vice are not essential for building the Ideal kit, they will save you a great deal of time.

You should have a screwdriver to fit each size of screw you use. The blade should be square at the end and the tip, to fit the slot in the screw head. With a properly fitting screwdriver you can hold a screw almost horizontally without it dropping off the screwdriver. A pump-action screwdriver is useful when driving in a large number of screws, as when fitting the rubbing strake.

The hitting face of a hammer should be clean and polished. You will also need a dolly to hammer against; an old iron weight would do very well.

Battery power tools are handy if working away from a power point.

Boat-building techniques

Building a boat is not as straightforward as making shelves or cupboards at home, because a boat is made up very largely of curved surfaces. Over the centuries, boat-builders have evolved a number

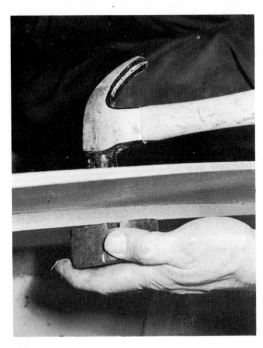

Plate 4: Using a dolly while hammering.

of techniques to make the job easier and quicker. Some of the more basic of these techniques are described below. If you are building your boat from a kit, you will not need to worry about marking out your timber from a set of drawings, but you are likely to find that you will use most of the others to some extent in the course of construction. Perhaps the most important single point to remember when building a boat is that it is not an exact, mechanical process; following instructions or drawings slavishly to the nearest fraction of a millimetre will never produce a good-looking boat. Use your eyes – what looks right, is right.

Marking out from plans

If your plans are drawn full size, then there is little problem in transferring the shapes to pieces of wood. Rectangular pieces can be drawn up by direct measurement, and curved shapes by means of carbon paper and a sharp point, or by pricking through the drawing on to the wood beneath. If the drawings are to a reduced scale, then things are a little more difficult. Rectangular pieces can still be measured, but the curved shapes have to be enlarged. The most accurate way of doing this is by constructing a grid over the drawing, and measuring off the co-ordinates of the shape where it crosses the grid (*Figure 4*). The co-ordinates of each point are then converted to full size and transferred to a corresponding grid on the piece of wood. Join up the series of points produced by means of a thin batten of wood, curved to pass through as many of the points as possible. The object is to produce a fair curve, so if a point lies somewhat off the line, ignore it (*Figure 5*). Some sets of drawings include a body plan and a table of offsets (*Figure 6*). The body plan is a series of half-sections of the hull at various distances from the bow (called stations). The table of offsets is a set of co-ordinates for these sections, worked out on a grid of horizontal lines called waterlines and vertical lines called buttocks. When marking out a

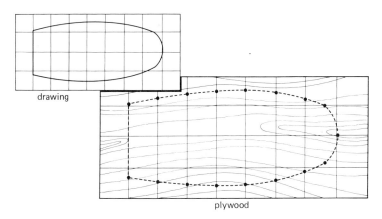

Figure 4: The co-ordinate method of enlarging curves.

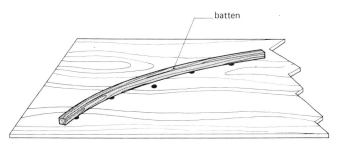

Figure 5: Using a batten to draw a fair curve. Points which do not fit the line are ignored.

bulkhead from a table of offsets, remember that the offsets refer to the outside dimensions of the hull, so the bulkhead must be reduced in size by an amount corresponding to the thickness of the skin.

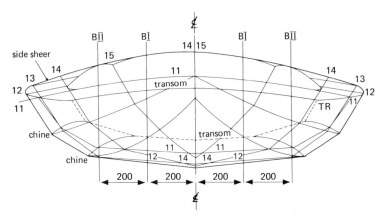

Figure 6: Body plan and table of offsets.

	Height from Baseline			½ Breadth from Centre Line				½ Br.	Height
Description	Transom	Frame 11	Frame 12	Frame 13	Frame 14	Frame 15	Stem		
Keel	—	—	—	—	—	—	—	x	
	165	117	76	55	65	105	—		x
Chine I	343	407	415	370	291	168	—	x	
	183	143	100	92	127	207	340		x
Chine II	456	554	593	553	434	250	—	x	
	240	215	193	200	242	316	430		x
Deck Side Sheer	505	640	697	671	552	330	—	x	
	325	338	355	384	423	470	520		x
Deck Mid Sheer	—	—	—	—	—	—	—	x	
	378	420	—	—	520	520	520		x
	—	—	—	—	—	—	—	x	
Buttock I	367 Deck	410 Deck			Deck 508	Deck 504			
	175	129	89	75	109	252	—		x
Buttock II	—	—	—	—	—	—		x	
	343 Deck	385 Deck			Deck 460				
	215	142	103	95	214	—	—		x
*Angled Side Deck	—	491	522	470	338	—	—	x	
	—	370	392	431	484	—	—		x
Angled Side Bh.d	—	407	415	370	291	—	—	x	
	—	310	322	370	447	—	—		x

Bevelling

When two pieces of wood meet at an angle, one of them must be bevelled to seat squarely on the other (*Figure 7*). There are several ways of taking off a bevel; by spiling (see below), or by the use of

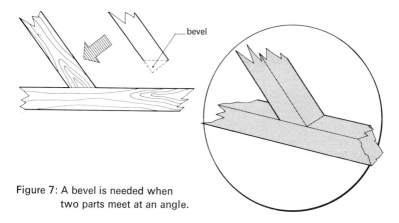

Figure 7: A bevel is needed when
two parts meet at an angle.

an adjustable bevel, either on the boat itself or on the drawing. In thin material like plywood, it is only necessary to mark off the bevel on the losing side, and plane off the edge by eye. For larger pieces, you must mark out the bevel carefully and use a saw or chisel. A good example of the use of bevels is the fitting of the bow and stern transoms and bulkheads to the keel plank of the Ideal dinghy (Chapter 6).

Spiling

It is often necessary to cut a piece of wood so that it fits exactly in place. Spiling is a way of marking out complicated shapes in a way that avoids a great deal of cut-and-try. The principle is shown in *Figure 8*. The piece of wood to be marked up is cut roughly to shape and laid as close to its final position as it will go. Then, using a

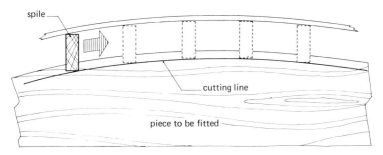

Figure 8: Using a spile to mark up a shape.

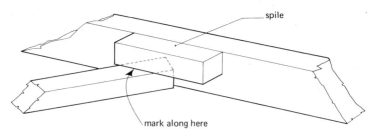

Figure 9: Using a spile to take off a bevel.

block of wood as a gauge, a line is drawn on the wood at a fixed distance from the fixed part. Cut the wood along this line, and it should fit exactly. Spiling is a neat and quick way of taking off a bevel (*Figure 9*). A variation on spiling is the useful marking gauge shown in *Figure 10*, which is used to mark a line for a series of fastenings, such as pins or screws to hold a deck in place.

Fairing

Fairing is the process of producing a smooth, fair surface on the boat so that it looks nice and moves easily through the water. Fairing is probably the most skilled of all boat-building techniques, but for the kit builder usually consists of little more than minor adjustments to make sure that the parts fit sweetly together. If you are building a boat in frame (see below), then fairing is more complicated, because you have to fair the basic framework of transom,

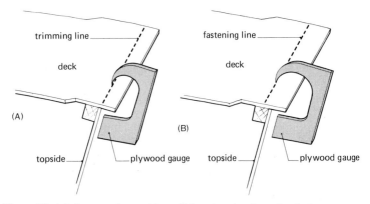

Figure 10: (*a*) A gauge for marking off the trimming line of a deck.
(*b*) A gauge for marking off a line for the deck fastenings.

hog, frames and longitudinals to provide a smooth surface for the skin to fit on to.

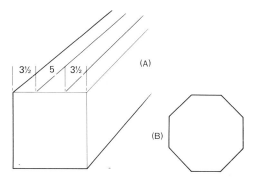

Figure 11: Rounding a spar; the spar is marked in the proportions $3\frac{1}{2}$:5:$3\frac{1}{2}$, as shown in (a). When the corners are planed off, the eight-sided figure (b) results. Each of these corners can be planed off, and the resulting shape smoothed to a round with sandpaper.

Rounding

It may be necessary for you to make a round mast or spar from a square piece of wood. The method to use is shown in *Figure 11*. First, make sure that the wood is accurately square in cross section, then mark two lines along each face, so that the face is divided in the proportion $3\frac{1}{2}$:5:$3\frac{1}{2}$. Plane off the corners to these lines to produce an eight-sided shape. Plane off each of these corners by eye to produce a sixteen-sided figure. Finally, smooth off the wood with sandpaper or a spokeshave to produce a round-sectioned mast.

Building in frame

In many modern plywood kit boats, including the Ideal, the skin is an integral part of the construction of the boat. Other boats require the construction of a rigid framework, consisting of the frames, transom, stem, hog and longitudinals. The skin is attached to this framework at a later stage. Such boats are said to be built 'in frame'. After the frames and transom have been cut out (often from a table of offsets), they are fixed in their correct relationship to the floor (the boat is built upside down). Then the hog, stem and longitudinals are fitted, to produce the rigid framework. This framework is carefully faired, and then the skin is fitted into place upon it. There is no doubt that building a boat in frame is more difficult than building a boat like the Ideal, but it is still within the powers of a fairly skilled home handyman.

5 Fixing Things Together

In the modern plywood dinghy, there are three main ways of fixing pieces of wood together, which can sometimes be used in combination with each other. They are:

Fasteners, such as nails and screws
Glue
Glass-fibre reinforced resin joints

Fasteners

There are several different types of fastening used in boat-building, which are chosen according to the nature of the joint and the function of the parts being joined. It may be necessary to make a joint that may be taken apart at some future time, or perhaps you just want to hold two pieces together until a glue line sets. Each job requires the correct fastener.

Screws

Perhaps the most widely used fastening in boats is the brass wood screw, which provides a very firm, positive joint. However, the wood screw is often used where it is not strictly necessary, and where an alternative fastener would save time, weight and money. Screws should be used in two circumstances; when it is likely that the part being fixed will be removed in the future, during refitting for example; or when it is desired to hold two parts firmly together against some form of resistance, as when holding a piece of wood in a curve.

Steel screws are never used in a boat, for the obvious reason that they will sooner or later rust and fail, but brass screws have the disadvantage of being soft. It is quite easy to twist a screw in half, and even easier to damage the slot in the head where the screwdriver goes. You should have a different screwdriver for each size of screw that you use, and the blade should fit the screw head properly (see 'Tools', page 25). The two main causes of difficulty in screwed joints are an unsuitable screwdriver and failure to drill the wood properly to receive the screws.

Drilling for a screw requires three different sizes of hole (*Figure 12*). This drilling is time-consuming, but should be done properly for all joints but those using small screws in very soft wood. Combination tools are available for power drills, which make all three holes at once, which saves a lot of time. The counterbore should be slightly larger than the diameter of the screw head, so that the screw can be driven without catching on the sides. Do not counterbore in thin plywood, but otherwise make sure the counterbore is deep enough. If the head of the screw is to be concealed by stopping or dowelling, then it should be at least two-thirds of its own diameter below the surface of the wood. Dowelling is a technique used in top-quality work that is to be varnished. A dowel, cut from the same wood as the part being fixed, is glued into the counterbore, with its grain lined up with the main part. After the glue is dry, the dowel is smoothed off level with the surface, and it becomes almost invisible. Special cutters are available to make dowels of different sizes.

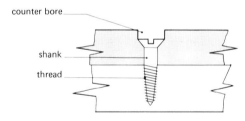

Figure 12: Drilling for screws.

The second hole, for the shank, should be a snug fit. If it is too slack, then water may be able to penetrate later on; on the other hand, the screw will be difficult to drive if this hole is too tight on the shank. The shank of the screw should go right through the top piece that is being fastened, as shown in *Figure 12*. You can control this by choosing screws with an appropriate length of shank, and then adjusting the depth of the counterbore.

It is important that the hole for the thread be the right size. Obviously, if it is too big, the threads will not bite into the wood, and the joint will be weak; to avoid this error, many people make the hole too small. Not only does this make the screw hard to drive, with the risk of breaking it; it also makes the joint weak, because the fibres of the wood are crushed and distorted by the screw. The proper action for a wood screw is for the threads to cut firmly into the wood of the bottom part, and then bring the pieces together by turning as a helical wedge.

When driving screws, a tiny spot of grease on the tip will make them easier to drive and easier to remove later on. Vaseline is ideal for this purpose, but do not use too much. If the head of the screw gets greasy, the screwdriver blade may slip and damage the screw. If the counterbore gets greasy, then the stopping or dowelling may not hold in place. Some people recommend putting glue on the screw thread, both to seal the hole and lock the screw permanently in place. If the joint in question is glued as well as screwed, then this extra sealing is unnecessary; and as you will not be able to take the screw out again after the glue has set, be quite sure that you have not made any mistake in the joint.

Table 2   Drilling sizes for screws

Screw size	Counterbore	Shank	Thread
5	$\frac{1}{4}$ in. (6·3 mm)	$\frac{1}{8}$ in. (3·1 mm)	bradawl
6	$\frac{5}{16}$ in. (7·9 mm)	$\frac{9}{64}$ in. (3·6 mm)	$\frac{5}{64}$ in. (2·0 mm)
8	$\frac{3}{8}$ in. (9·5 mm)	$\frac{11}{64}$ in. (4·4 mm)	$\frac{3}{32}$ in. (2·4 mm)
10	$\frac{7}{16}$ in. (11·1 mm)	$\frac{7}{32}$ in. (5·6 mm)	$\frac{7}{64}$ in. (2·8 mm)

Copper boat nails

Copper nails can be used for light work, especially as a temporary fastening for a glued joint. They are very soft and are easily bent. Drill a pilot hole for the nail, about half its diameter. Do not try to straighten a bent nail, because it will almost certainly bend again. Throw it away, and use a new nail in a slightly bigger pilot hole. When used to fasten thin sheets of wood together, as in a butt strap joint in plywood, copper nails can be clenched, as shown in *Figure 13*, to make them bite firmly.

Panel pins

Brass panel pins are widely used in the building of plywood dinghies, to hold pieces together while a glued joint sets. Drilling for panel

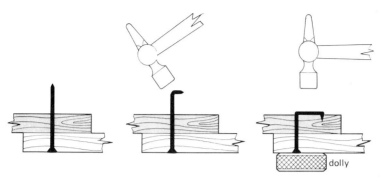

Figure 13: Clenching a nail.

pins is not normally necessary, except in very hard wood, but a pilot hole can be helpful in getting the pin started in the right place and holding it for the first blow of the hammer. Do not drive the pin so far that the face of the hammer actually hits the wood; this can squeeze glue out from between the two pieces of wood, leading to a glue-starved joint. You should drive the pin with the hammer until the head is just above the surface, and then drive it flush with the surface by using a pin punch. If you prefer, you can drive the head of the pin below the surface with the pin punch, and stop the hole up afterwards. Be careful not to do this too vigorously if the top part of the joint is thin plywood, as it is possible to push the head of the pin right through, making the joint useless.

Barbed ring nails

Barbed ring nails can sometimes be used instead of screws. They are nails with a series of barbs on the shank, like those on a fish hook or a harpoon. The nails can be driven in like any other nail, but the barbs then grip the wood and prevent the nail coming out again. They are lighter and cheaper than screws, but are very much harder to get out.

Glues

The introduction of modern waterproof glues has revolutionized boatbuilding methods. When used properly, a glued joint can be stronger than the wood itself. Given a few simple precautions, the amateur can trust his glued joints absolutely. Most marine glues are described as 'gap filling', which means that the glue will fill up small errors in the joint. But this should not be taken as a licence to be careless in the fitting of joints; the gap-filling ability is limited, and you should still make your joints fit as accurately as you can.

There are three main types of glue which can be used in boat construction, each based on a different group of chemicals. They are all made in two parts, a resin and a hardener. Some glues require these two components to be mixed together before use; with others, the resin is applied to one of the parts to be joined and the hardener to the other, so that the glue does not begin to set until after the two parts have been brought together.

The three types of glue are urea (Aerolite 306, Cascamite), resorcinol (Aerodux, Cascophen) and epoxy (Araldite). Of these, the urea glues are almost invariably specified for amateur boat-building, so they will be dealt with first and in the greatest detail.

Aerolite 306 urea–formaldehyde glue

Aerolite 306 is a two-part adhesive; a resin, which is supplied in powder form, and a liquid hardener. It is described as a gap-filling, water-resistant adhesive, unaffected by moulds and fungi. It was used to glue the wooden Mosquito bomber together during the Second World War, which is probably as good a recommendation as you can get. Equally important from the amateur's point of view is the fact that it is relatively cheap and very easy to use.

The powdered resin is mixed with water to form a syrupy liquid. The approximate proportions are two parts of powder to one part of water (by weight), or four parts of powder to one part of water (by volume). Use a dry, non-metallic container and add the water to the powder gradually, stirring well to prevent lumps. Continue stirring after all the water has been added until the resin is completely dissolved. Warm water (20–35°C) assists in the process. If you are able, let the solution stand after mixing, to allow any bubbles to disperse. The mixed resin has a life of about two weeks, so do not mix up more than you can use in this time. The dry powder has a shelf life of two years at least.

To use Aerolite, first make sure that the surfaces to be joined are clean, dry and free of dust, and that the joint fits as well as you can make it. Apply the resin to the smaller of the two pieces by means of a spreader or brush. Then apply the hardener to the other surface with a pad or sponge, using enough to make the wood uniformly damp. Now put the two pieces together, make sure they are in the correct position, and then hold them firmly together with clamps, weights or panel pins.

The two pieces must be held together firmly, so that there is no possibility of them moving, but the joint should not be over-clamped, which would squeeze the glue out of the joint and lead to starvation and weakness. It takes a little practice to judge how much resin to apply. You have got it right when a small bead of resin oozes out all round the joint as you clamp it up. Too much is better than too little, provided that you clean off the surplus before it sets. In making a long joint, as when fixing a rubbing strake along the gunwhale for example, it is possible for the hardener to dry out before you get round to clamping the far end. If there are signs that this might happen, re-apply hardener to the dry areas before clamping.

There are two times of importance in gluing. One is called 'shuffling time', and is the length of time that you can move the two pieces about after bringing the resin and hardener together. The clamps must be applied before the shuffling time is up. The other time is called 'clamping time', and is the minimum time needed for the glue to set and develop reasonable strength. Both these times depend on the hardener in use and the temperature, as is shown in *Table 3*.

Table 3   Aerolite 306 – shuffling and clamping times

Hardener	Temperature (°C)				
	10	15	20	25	30
GBQ.X Shuffling	30 min.	20 min.	10 min.	5 min.	—
Clamping	5–6 hr	$2\frac{3}{4}$ hr	$1\frac{3}{4}$ hr	$1\frac{1}{4}$ hr	1 hr
GBP.X Shuffling	—	25 min.	15 min.	10 min.	5 min.
Clamping	—	$3\frac{1}{2}$ hr	$2\frac{1}{4}$ hr	$1\frac{1}{2}$ hr	$1\frac{1}{4}$ hr

As *Table 3* shows, the two setting times are very dependent upon temperature. Two things follow from this. Firstly, it is possible to speed up the work by applying local heating to a glued joint to make it set more quickly; do not overdo this, however, or you may cause cracking in the wood or in the glued joint. The other consequence is the need to keep the temperature of the glue line at a reasonable value; if glue is left to set overnight in an unheated shed in the wintertime, it would be wise to provide local heating. A large light bulb under some sort of cover will generally be enough to keep the temperature reasonable.

There are a number of points to watch in the use of Aerolite 306. Neither the resin nor the hardener should be allowed to come into contact with iron or steel, whether in containers, on brushes or applicators, or on the boat itself. Staining of the wood may result, which can be difficult to remove. The wood being joined should not be damp; the makers recommend a moisture content of 7 to 13 per cent, which implies kiln-dried wood, but air-dried wood will glue perfectly well. Excess glue should be removed from the joint, either immediately with a damp cloth, or after it has set to a rubbery state with a scraper. If surplus glue is allowed to harden, it is almost impossible to remove and it will blunt tools and may spoil the appearance. After gluing, mixers and spreaders can be cleaned in warm water.

The resin is quite harmless to people, as long as sensible standards of care and cleanliness are observed. The hardener contains formic acid, which is corrosive; it is the substance used by ants when they sting. The hardener must not be swallowed or allowed to come in contact with the eyes or the skin. If it gets in the eyes, hold the eyelids open and flush them thoroughly with water, then seek medical attention at once. Acid on the skin should be washed off with soap and warm water; contaminated clothing should be washed before it is worn again.

Cascamite one-shot glue

This is the brand name of another urea–formaldehyde glue, which is supplied as a powder containing both resin and hardener. The powder is made up with water, which activates the hardener so that the glue begins to set; you should not mix up more glue than you can use in the relatively short time before it sets. At 15°C, the glue has a pot life of about three hours and a shuffling time of 25 minutes. Both these times are reduced at higher temperatures.

Resorcinol glues

Resorcinol glues are supplied with the resin and hardener pre-mixed. They have a superior performance to urea–formaldehyde glues, but are harder to use and more expensive. They are more suited for professional use. Resorcinol glues should not be used at temperatures below 20°C, which means that local heating is almost always necessary.

Epoxy glues

Epoxy resin glues, such as Araldite and Araldite Rapid, are versatile and powerful adhesives which will stick almost anything to almost anything. They are supplied as a resin and a hardener in separate tubes which have to be mixed together before use. Though excellent glues, they are too expensive to be used on a wide scale in boatbuilding, but Araldite Rapid in particular can be very useful for a quick repair when away from home.

PVA glues

These are common woodworking glues sold in hardware shops and DIY stores. They require no hardener and are cheap and easy to use, but their resistance to water and fungal attack is not good enough for use in the structural parts of a boat.

Glass-fibre reinforced resin joints

Many modern plywood dinghies, including the Ideal, use glass-fibre reinforced resin joints to hold the skin panels together. These joints are simple and efficient, they add strength to the boat and they are completely watertight. The joint is made up of two components; a transparent, syrupy resin, rather like a thick varnish, and a tape about 2 in. (5 cm) wide woven from glass fibres. When a catalyst is added to the resin, it sets hard in about half an hour. It is strong but brittle. The function of the tape is to reinforce the resin, in the same way that steel rods are used to reinforce concrete in civil engineering.

The first step in making the joint is to make sure that the edges to be joined are clean and dry, and fit together reasonably well. Then cut lengths of the tape to fit the joints you intend to make. Treat the tape with care, as it tends to unravel at the ends, and put it somewhere close by the job. Put on some gloves, or rub barrier cream into your hands, and you are ready for the resin.

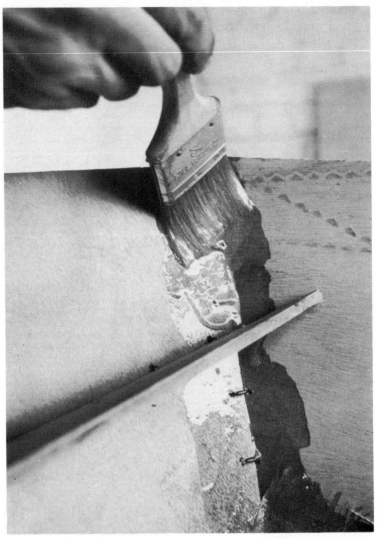

Plate 5: Applying resin to a joint.

The resin needs a catalyst or hardener to make it go solid. The normal proportion is about $\frac{3}{4}$ per cent catalyst, though fast or slow mixtures can be made using 1 or $\frac{1}{2}$ per cent catalyst. At normal temperatures, a $\frac{3}{4}$ per cent mix will go off in about half an hour. Pour about $\frac{1}{2}$ Kg of resin into an empty food tin or other scrap container,

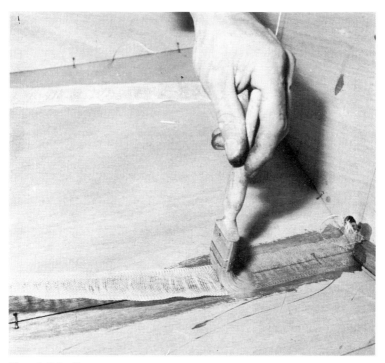

Plate 6: Stippling resin into glass-fibre tape.

and add 3·75 cc, or a little less than two teaspoonfuls, of the catalyst. Treat the catalyst with caution, as it is a fairly unpleasant chemical, and stir it well into the resin. Keep stirring from time to time throughout the operation.

Take a brush, and paint a strip of resin, a little wider than the tape, along the whole length of the joint. You will find that it behaves rather like sticky varnish. Then pick up the length of tape and lay it carefully along the joint, on top of the wet resin, making sure that it lies flat and even. Now put some more resin in the brush, and work your way along the tape, stippling resin thoroughly into the weave of the tape so that it becomes completely impregnated with resin. This process is known as 'wetting out' the tape. The tape must be made to lie flat and even with no trace of gaps or air bubbles underneath, which give a milky appearance. The tape tends to slip about and stick to the brush, so care and patience is required to get a perfect joint, especially when the panels meet in an angle.

After wetting out the first joint, you can go on to another, returning later to give another quick coat of resin to the first. When the tape has been properly wetted out, it becomes almost invisible, and the joint looks as though it has merely been given a very heavy coat of varnish.

If the resin in the tin starts to go lumpy, then throw it away at once and wash out your brush in the special solvent (acetone). The resin gives off heat as it gels, and if you delay too long you will find yourself holding a tin of very hot rock, with a brush permanently embedded in it. With the correct proportion of hardener, you should be able to use up the whole tinful before it goes off. If you have any left over, do not waste it – give the seams you have already done another coat of resin for luck. The resin should set in about half an hour, but the surface will feel slightly tacky for several days. If the resin fails to set, then you have put in too little catalyst, or you are working at too low a temperature. Correct whatever is wrong, and put on another coat of resin, which will make the original application set as well.

When you have finished, wash out the brush in acetone. Work some into the bristles, then discard the acetone and repeat with a fresh lot. But however careful you may be with your resin brush, it will only have a limited life; it will not be long before setting resin accumulates and makes the brush useless. Remember, too, that acetone is inflammable.

6 Building the Ideal

This chapter describes in general terms the various stages in assembling the Ideal dinghy. These are not the detailed building instructions (which are supplied with the kit), but a condensed summary to demonstrate how much is involved in the construction of a modern plywood dinghy.

On receiving your kit, check the packing for signs of damage; if you find any, sign the carrier's delivery note to that effect. Then unpack the kit and check the contents carefully against the parts list. Notify the supplier if you find anything missing or broken. Then put the wooden parts away until needed, as described at the end of Chapter 3.

Generally speaking, you should follow the order of assembly given in the instructions, but if space is at a premium, then you can make all the small parts first; it takes no more work to make them early on, and the working space is not cluttered by the hull of the boat. The Ideal is 12 ft 3 in. (3·7 m) long and has a beam of 5 ft 3 in. (1·6 m), so it takes up a reasonable amount of floor space. You need a workshop area about the size of the average garage in which to build it. If building a boat indoors, do make certain before you begin that you will be able to get it out when you have finished it.

Making up transoms and bulkheads

The bulkheads and transoms are made of sheets of ply, which need to be reinforced at the edges so they can be fixed to the hull, and so that other parts can be fixed to them. The two bulkheads and the stern transom need to be bevelled, so that they will stand correctly on the keel plank as assembly progresses (*Figure 14*). The fore transom is curved roughly into shape by being wired to a jig supplied with the kit.

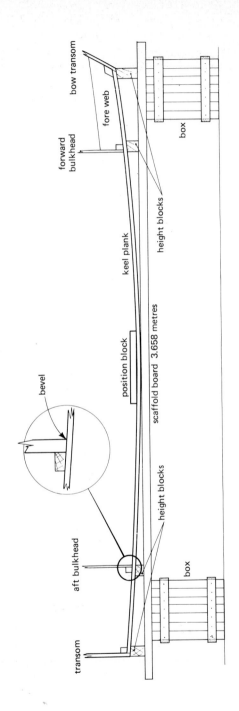

Figure 14: The Ideal in building stocks.

Other small parts are assembled at this stage; the centreboard case, the sides of the centre buoyancy tank and the web which fits between the bow transom and the forward bulkhead. These are also plywood parts which need stiffening and support at the edges. In all cases the stiffening parts are glued and pinned to the plywood.

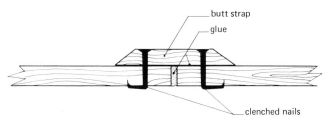

Figure 15: A butt strap joint.

Jointing the planking

As the Ideal is over 12 ft (3·7 m) long, and plywood comes in 8 × 4 ft (2·4 × 1·2 m) sheets, it is necessary to make up the skin panels from two pieces which must be joined together. There are five hull panels altogether – the keel plank, two bilge planks and two topside planks. They are all joined in a similar way, using a butt strap joint (*Figure 15*). The two parts of each plank are put together and glued, with the butt strap glued and pinned over the joint. The pins holding the butt strap should be clenched (Chapter 5), and you should make sure that the gap between the ends of the planks is well filled with glue to protect the end grain of the plywood. When joining the two topside planks, the butt strap should stop a little short of the top edge, to allow for the fitting of the gunwale later on.

Assembling the hull

The assembly of the hull can now begin, and it is helpful to make up a set of building stocks as shown in *Figure 14*. No elaborate devices to hold parts in position are needed, because the boat falls naturally into shape as it is put together. The first step is to mark out the keel plank, the positions of the transom, the fore transom block, the fore web and the two bulkheads. The position of the centreboard case is also marked, and holes are drilled for the fixing screws for all these parts. Also drill small holes around the edge of the keel plank for the wire stitches that will hold the bilge planks on to it.

At this stage, it is worth fitting up all these parts on the keel plank dry (i.e. without glue). All parts should sit fairly on the plank, the bulkheads and transom should be at right angles to the fore-and-aft line, and they should be vertical when the plank is mounted on the stocks. If all is well, the parts can be fixed permanently into position.

The first part to fix is the centreboard case; turn the keel plank upside down and check that the bottom surface of the case sits fairly on it. Glue and screw the case in position, using plenty of glue to make sure that any small inequality is filled. Then glue and screw similarly the transom, the two bulkheads, the fore web and the bow transom, still bent round its jig. Turn the keel plank the right way up (you will need some help), set it up on the stocks, and check that all the parts are correctly positioned. Wipe off any surplus glue and nail light battens to support each of the parts and protect them from accidental damage until the planking takes over.

Now fit the bilge planks in place with wire stitches. First, drill small holes for the stitching along the edge of the transom. You will need a helper to hold the bilge plank on one side in its proper position, while you drill holes in it to match those on the transom and keel plank. Put in wire stitches loosely to hold the bilge plank in place, working from the stern up as far as the forward bulkhead. Repeat the process for the bilge plank on the other side. Take care always to treat both sides of the boat exactly alike.

The next stage is the most difficult in assembling the hull. The bilge planks have to be wired to the keel plank up to the bow transom in a curve, which puts strain on the plywood. Use extra stitches where it seems necessary. The forward end of the bilge planks is stitched to the bow transom, which may need some adjustment of its curvature.

The topside panels can now be wired in place in a similar way. Start on one quarter, work your way up to the forward bulkhead; then put on the panel on the other side, all the way to the bow, and return to finish off the first panel.

The hull is now completely skinned and ready for the glass-fibre resin reinforced joints (Chapter 5). First, the two topside stringers are slipped into position, then the boat is lined up ready for the glass tape and resin. The wire stitches holding the hull must be gradually tightened until the planks are seated firmly against each

Plate 7: Stephen Atkinson shows the Ideal dinghy kit that he put together
in the Ulster Television series *Build Your Own Boat*.

other with the smallest gaps possible between them. At the same time,
the boat must sit firmly on the building stocks and be upright and
without twist ('out of wind', as the boat-builders say). A few strat-
egically placed sandbags can help hold the boat down on the stocks.
Once the stitches are tight and the hull is in its proper position, it
should be held there by four wooden legs. If, during this lining up
process, you feel that some extra stitches are needed, then put them
in.

Now you can put on the resin and glass-fibre tape; first press the
wire stitches into the corners, flush with the wood. Then resin and

Plate 8: Centreboard case sides made up and painted.

Plate 9: The centreboard case complete.

Plate 10: The two sides of a butt strap joint.

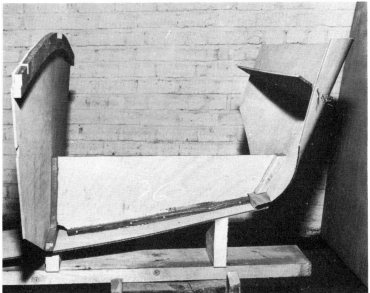

Plate 11: The bow transom, fore web and main bulkhead fitted to the keel plank. Note the jig wired to the bow transom to hold it in a curve.

tape all the internal corners where ply meets ply without a supporting block. A useful tip before resining is to put PVC tape along the outside of the joints, between the stitches. This tape prevents resin dribbling through the joint and consequently makes the resin fill the joint completely. The hull should not be disturbed until the resin has set completely.

Finishing the hull

Now comes a succession of small jobs; the midships and stern buoyancy tanks have to be fitted, and the insides painted with a primer and at least one other coat of paint. The bow buoyancy tank can be painted at this time, too. All chips and sawdust should be removed before painting, and you should not paint surfaces which will later be glued. Then the aft deck and the midships tank top can be fitted, after painting their under side and fitting the watertight hatch. The mast step can then be fixed on top of the midships buoyancy tank at the forward end.

The top edge of the boat is now stiffened by fixing the inwhales along the inside top edge of the topsides, the transom top beam along the transom, and three curved pieces of ply, one on top of the other, round the top of the bow transom. These latter parts are glued and held by clenched nails. Their top surface will need fairing after the glue has set. Five brackets must be fixed on each topside to support the side decks and side benches; the forward of these brackets also provides an anchorage for the shroud chainplates.

Next, the supports for the foredeck and the side decks must be fitted. The king plank runs from the bow transom to a little way aft of the forward bulkhead, on the centre line. The foredeck beam is a curved athwartships beam fitted between the bow transom and the forward bulkhead. The side deck carlins support the inboard edges of the side deck, and run from the forward bulkhead right aft to the transom. There are two angled carlins which support the fore deck where it projects aft of the forward bulkhead.

Decking

Now comes the critical job of decking the boat. It is critical because in no other aspect of boat-building is the builder's skill or carelessness more obvious than in the way he has put the decks on. First,

Plate 12: The inside of a wired joint.

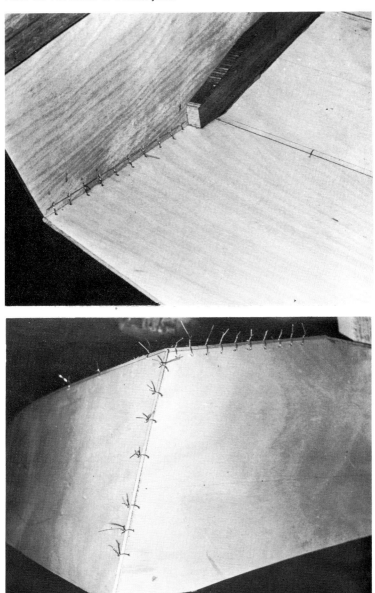

Plate 13: Wired joints from the outside.

Plate 14: Bulkheads, transoms and centreboard case in place. The bilge panels have been fitted. Note the jig across the centreboard case to hold the topside panels in the correct curve.

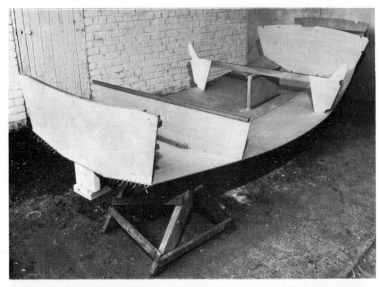

Plate 15: The centre buoyancy tank ready for capping.

use a plane to make all the top edges of the beams and carlins really fair with each other. Test them with a straight-edge and a flexible batten (on curves), to make sure that the plywood deck will sit firmly on them. The decks will not be strong if they are badly supported, and the watertight integrity of the forward buoyancy tank depends on the quality of the joint around the deck.

The deck panels should be arranged so that their better faces are uppermost. The side decks should be fitted first, and the foredeck halves butted up to them. Deck panels are supplied oversize, so they can be trimmed after they have been fitted. Paint the underside of the foredeck and pin and glue it in place. Then pin and glue the side decks. Use a spiling gauge to mark the trimming line for the deck, and a line for the fastening pins (Chapter 4). When sawing off the overhang, use a fine, sharp saw to avoid chipping the face veneers.

Finishing touches

The inside of the hull needs a few finishing touches; floor battens have to be fixed to the bilge panels, to give a grip for the feet, and the rubbing strake and transom capping have to be put on. When

Plate 16: The Ideal dinghy ready for resin and glass fibre.

Plate 17: The aft buoyancy tank ready for decking.

Plate 18: Side deck and side bench knees in position.

Plate 19: Side deck
carlins in place.

gluing and screwing the rubbing strake, start at one end, and work your way steadily along the length of the boat, one screw at a time, until you reach the other end. A pump-action screwdriver is useful for this job, but beware of the hardener drying out of the wood before you reach the far end. Apply more hardener if necessary. The rowlock chocks also have to be fitted.

Finishing the outside

The boat can now be turned over, and the outside cleaned up. The copper stitches can be removed (in fact, they can be removed as soon as the resin has set; it makes working on the boat more comfortable), and the corners cleaned off with a file or surform. Take care not to damage the veneers. When the corners have been cleaned up and rounded, glass-fibre tape and resin are applied to all the joints; take care to wet out the tape thoroughly and make it lie flat. On an obtuse-angled joint, the tape tends to lift. Give the joints a few extra coats of resin to fill up the pattern of the mesh, so that the finished surface will be smoother. Finally, the two chine beads can be fitted

Plate 20: Using a batten to test the fairness of the fore deck supports.

Plate 21: The outside of the boat ready for glass-fibre tape and resin.

Plate 22: The Ideal dinghy ready for sanding and painting.

along the edges of the keel plank the whole length of the boat. These beads are screwed in place, and can be seated either on glue or on resin.

Finally, clean out the boat, remove all dribbles of resin, ends of tape and so on, both inside and out, fit the side benches, and start to prepare the boat for painting and varnishing (Chapter 7).

The basic Ideal is now complete, but a few details remain. Various accessories have to be assembled and finished, the rudder, tiller, centreboard and gaff. And the fittings have to be screwed firmly in place. By the time you have finished putting them all on, you will be aware just how many screws there are in a small boat!

7 Painting and Varnishing

The final stage in the completion of the hull is painting and varnishing, which has two functions. First, and most important, it gives the surface of the wood a hard, smooth, waterproof covering which protects the wood and keeps it dry. Secondly, it makes the boat look attractive. Painting and varnishing are slow processes, but are worth doing well; the life of the boat, as well as its final appearance, depends very much on the protection given by a thin layer of paint.

Before painting can begin, the whole boat must be sanded thoroughly to remove roughness and whiskers of wood. Every surface should be as smooth as you can possibly make it. For hand sanding, wrap the sandpaper round a cork block because uneven pressure from the fingers can cause more wood to be removed from some areas than from others, making the surface irregular. Sand with the grain of the wood, as cross sanding tends to tear the surface fibres, leading to a rougher finish. For large areas, an orbital sander can save a great deal of work, but a final light sanding by hand is recommended, to remove the circular scratches left by the orbital sander. Avoid the use of a disc sander on a power tool; it tends to leave deep semi-circular marks on the surface which are very difficult to remove.

While painting, you must keep the whole area scrupulously clean and free of dust. Sweep up all the shavings, vacuum clean the whole area thoroughly, and wipe the boat with a rag dipped in white spirit to remove dust from the grain of the wood. Wear clothes that will not shed dust or hairs over everything, and discourage visitors – especially the dog. It is remarkable how much irritation and frustration a clean working space can save.

Types of paint

There are three types of paint available for painting small boats: synthetic marine paint, one-part polyurethane paint, and two-part polyurethane paint. The polyurethanes have some advantages over synthetic paint, but they are harder to use. The newcomer would be wise to stick to the more conventional material and this chapter assumes that synthetic marine paints are being used. If you do decide to try the polyurethanes, read the instructions carefully and follow them to the letter. There are several reputable manufacturers of marine paints, and from the amateur's point of view there is little to choose between them. There are technical differences which make it wise to stick to the products of one manufacturer while going through the various stages of painting; when repainting later, you may change to another brand if you wish.

Priming and filling

The first coat of paint is a priming coat which seals the pores of the wood and provides a foundation for subsequent coats. A generous coat of metallic pink primer should be brushed well into the grain of the wood, and into every crack and corner. Do not skimp on this coat, but on the other hand do not put on so much primer that it starts to run. Read the instructions on the tin before you start (the golden rule of painting), and pay particular attention to stirring the paint.

When the primer is dry, fill in all the depressions, holes and cracks on the surface to be painted with the best quality waterproof filler. If there are any big holes to fill, it might be better to use a resin putty, such as Isopon, which is stronger than a filler. Large holes should be filled in stages, because the filler tends to shrink as it dries. Fillers should be applied with a broad-bladed flexible knife, and should be left to dry thoroughly.

Next, sand the boat again, both to make the areas you have just filled smooth and level with the surface, and to remove all the imperfections that you missed on your first sanding; the primer coat will make them glaringly obvious. Do not worry if this sanding takes you back to bare wood in places; merely touch up these spots with primer when you have finished sanding.

Undercoats

The next step is to apply two (or more) coats of undercoat. An undercoat is a paint which contains a great deal of pigment. It is designed to provide the solid background of colour for the top coat, which dries to a high gloss, but has very little pigment and hence poor covering power. The undercoat has excellent covering power, but dries to a matt finish. As a thick paint, it has an added bonus for the amateur, in that it acts rather like a filler as well, making the surface smoother than it might otherwise be. It is not usual to thin an undercoat (read the instructions on the tin), and it is essential to stir it very well indeed. The mass of pigment in the paint settles relatively quickly and if the tin has been standing on the chandler's shelf for any length of time, the pigment will have formed an almost solid mass at the bottom of the tin. It helps to turn the tin upside down a few days before you use it, to get the pigment moving again. Stir thoroughly with a flat piece of wood (not something round) and go on stirring until the paint is of a smooth, even consistency throughout the tin. If you have an electric drill, you can buy a paint stirring attachment, which is very good. Undercoat should be applied generously and brushed well in; when it is dry, rub it down with wet-or-dry paper, used wet (see below). Two undercoats should be sufficient, but if you are very fussy, you may want to apply a third.

Wet-or-dry

The technique of rubbing down a coat of paint to make it smooth and provide a key for the next coat is very different from sanding a wooden surface. Use waterproof abrasive paper, known as wet-or-dry, and keep on dipping it in water as you are using it (warm water is kinder to the hands). The purpose of the water is to lubricate the cutting action of the paper and to prevent the paper from clogging. It does not matter if the surface you are painting gets wet, because it is by now protected by earlier coats of paint. Hold the wet-or-dry in your hand and rub lightly over the surface with your finger-tips. After a little practice, your fingers will be able to feel the irregularities on the surface through the paper. Work steadily over the whole surface, wetting the paper often. Wet-or-dry is expensive, but will last an amazingly long time if used properly. When used on paint, 240 grade gives a fairly coarse cut, 320 grade a medium cut and 400 grade a fine cut. When you have finished rubbing down, mop the surface clean and leave it to dry before attempting to put on the next coat of paint.

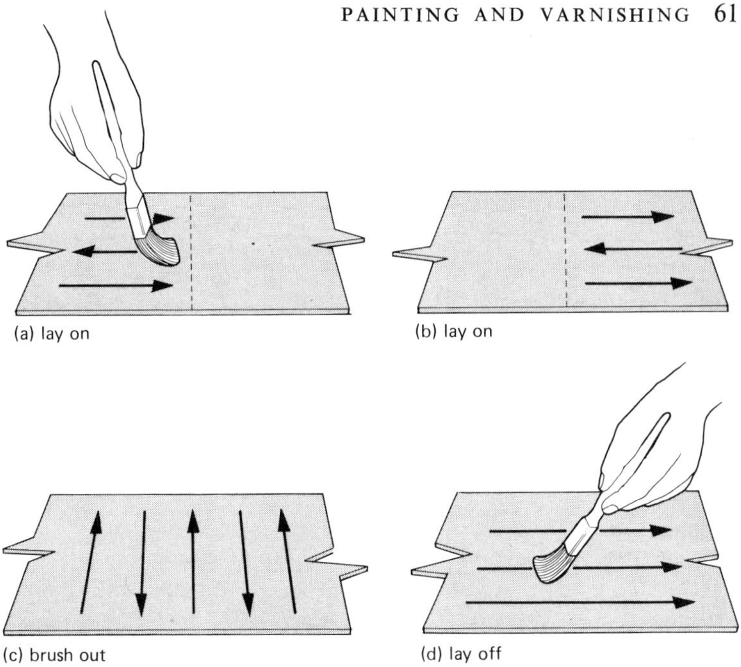

(a) lay on (b) lay on

(c) brush out (d) lay off

Figure 16: Laying on, brushing out and laying off.

The top coat

The top coat is the one that gives the boat its final gloss, and sets off all the hard work that you have put into building and painting it. Redouble your precautions against dust and fluff, and make sure that the surface that you have built up from sanding, priming, undercoating and rubbing down is as perfect as you can make it. One coat of enamel ought to be enough, but two will give better protection; a second coat is well worth putting on.

Charge the brush with paint, and then brush the paint over a small area, using lengthways (fore and aft) strokes (*Figure 16*). Repeat the process for an adjacent area, then work the paint well into both areas by brushing at right angles to the original application. Finally, brush with feather-light, delicate strokes in the original direction, to remove any brush marks. This process is called 'laying off' and is the secret of a high gloss finish.

It may be necessary to thin the top coat (but see what it says on the tin). A brush that drags over the paint is a sign that thinning might be needed. Add about 5 to 10 per cent of the correct thinner to the paint and stir it well in. Another cause of a dragging brush may lie in the brush itself. In good drying conditions, the paint can start to dry in the bristles of the brush; a few drops of thinners worked well into the bristles will soon take care of that. If the brush feels as though it is sliding across the surface, then you are probably putting on too much paint. Carry a rag moistened in thinners in the other hand, to mop up splashes and spills immediately. Remove nibs and hairs from the newly painted surface at once, but do not worry about the swarms of small flies which seem to find a fatal attraction in new paint. After the paint has dried, you will be able to brush the flies off, leaving barely a mark behind. Always paint a complete panel at one session; if you leave a panel half painted and finish it later, the join will always be obvious.

Varnishing

It is conventional to paint the outside of a plywood dinghy's hull and varnish the inside, though it is, of course, entirely up to you. Varnish is applied in essentially the same way as paint, but with one or two important differences. As varnish is transparent, the wood surface underneath it must be as perfect as possible. Any filler you have used should be coloured to match the wood. As many woods change colour when varnished, put a little varnish on a scrap piece of the same wood, and match the filler to the resulting colour.

A second difference between varnish and paint is that it is clearly impossible to prime a surface that is to be varnished. Instead, put on a coat of varnish thinned with 25 to 30 per cent white spirit; this will seal the surface of the wood in the same way that a primer does. Subsequent coats of varnish should be put on unthinned, rubbing down with wet-or-dry between each. You will need at least two coats of unthinned varnish, but you can put on as many as you like, until the surface is to your satisfaction. Four or five coats are quite common.

Brushes

Buy the very best brushes you can afford, and look after them carefully; you will need a 2 in. (5 cm) brush for the large surfaces and a 1 in. (2·5 cm) brush for the corners and edges. Every new brush seems to have a few loose bristles in it; before you use it for the first time, rub it a few times across a sheet of coarse sandpaper to remove any loose bristles and stop them going on your newly painted surface later. There is no need to clean out a brush at the end of a day's work if you intend to go on painting the next day. Stand the brush in a jar of water so that the bristles are covered, and it will remain soft until you use it again. When you resume painting, shake off the water and put a few brushfuls of paint on to a piece of scrap wood, then carry on painting.

To clean a brush, first scrape as much paint as you can back into the tin. Then work the brush well in thinners, paying particular attention to the roots of the bristles. Then repeat the process in fresh thinners. To complete the process, I then squirt washing-up liquid into the bristles and work it well in, and finish off by rinsing the brush in lukewarm water. When a brush has been properly cleaned, it should not be possible to tell what colour paint has been used in it.

Keeping paint

You should arrange to have a little paint left over when you have finished painting your boat, for touching up purposes. Clean out any paint that has run into the rim around the top of the can, put a circle of greaseproof paper over the surface of the paint, and push the lid on firmly. This prevents air getting in and forming a skin over the surface of the paint. If, in spite of your best endeavours, there is a skin on the paint when you want to use it again, then cut round the skin with a sharp knife and remove it – in one piece if possible. Then stir the paint and strain it through an old nylon stocking into a clean tin.

8 Moving the Boat

Unless you are lucky enough to have a river at the bottom of your garden, you will need to move the boat to a suitable stretch of water before you can use it. This almost certainly means that you will want to move the boat by car on the public roads. There are two ways of doing this: by putting it on a roof rack, or putting it on a trailer.

Roof racks

There are few problems in car-topping a boat, provided that you make sure that both roof rack and the car roof are strong enough for the job; there are obvious dangers if either of them should fail while you are driving along. Nor should you put too much top weight on the car roof, as this can make it unstable. Quite apart from the dangers arising from overloading and the risk of prosecution, you may find that your car insurance is made invalid. In calculating top weight, remember to add in the weight of the roof rack itself and the boat's gear.

The best type of roof rack for a boat is called a ladder rack, and consists merely of two tubes across the car. In any event, do not use the conventional luggage rack which has sides fitted to it; it is almost impossible to support the boat properly on such a rack. Put the boat on the rack upside down, so that as you drive along the wind forces tend to push the boat down, rather than lift it up. The job of putting it on (or taking it off) is best done by three people, though two can manage it if necessary. Turn the boat upside down behind the car on some padding. Then, with one person at the stern and the other two on each bow, by the chainplates, lift the boat up and walk it over the car. Make sure that the boat fits snugly on the rack, and pad the supporting points well. Fasten the boat on the rack firmly with webbing straps and tie the bow and stern down

Plate 23: The Ideal dinghy on a car roof rack.

securely to the front and rear bumper bar brackets. The object is to make sure that the boat will not move forwards, backwards, or sideways, and will not bounce up and down on the rack while you are driving. When you have loaded the rack, check the fixings that attach the roof rack to the car. They may have become slack as the load came on, and they should be tightened evenly.

The weight of the boat on the roof of the car will raise the centre of gravity, so drive carefully and avoid violent acceleration, braking or cornering. Anything that projects more than 3 ft (1 m) to the rear must be marked (see *Regulations*).

Plate 24: The author, with the Ideal on a road trailer.

Trailers

It is vital to ensure that the trailer is safely and securely attached to the car. A proper towing hitch must be fitted, and should be looked after properly. There are various types of hitch, but the modern standard is the 50 mm ball hitch, which you should use if you can. In any case, it is vital that the same type of hitch is fitted to both the car and the trailer. In particular, it is very dangerous to tow a trailer with the old 2 in. ball socket behind a car with a 50 mm ball. They may appear to fit, but might come apart on the road. The police would regard such a combination as a dangerous load.

Make sure that the boat fits snugly on the trailer. A boat's hull is designed to be evenly supported by water, so prevent the load coming on just a few points, because they are likely to fail and cause damage to the boat. If your trailer cannot be adjusted satisfactorily, then it is worth buying or making special chocks to fit the boat. Lash the boat down well, so that it cannot move or bounce about.

Driving with a trailer is straightforward enough when you are going forward, but is a bit more exciting in reverse! To make the trailer turn while reversing, you have to steer the car in the opposite direction to begin with, and then follow the trailer round. It takes a bit of practice to get it right and avoid the dreaded jacknife. Get some confidence by trying your hand in a nice empty, open space before you attempt to do it in public.

The balance of the boat and its gear on the trailer is of considerable importance. The load should be adjusted to give the correct nose weight, or weight on the towing hitch. The correct nose weight for your car should be given in the maker's handbook. An incorrect nose weight can cause the trailer to snake and affect the handling of the car.

It is not advisable to run a road trailer into the water to launch the boat, as the wheel bearings will not enjoy getting wet. Whenever possible, you should use a launching trolley, but if you are forced to put the road trailer in the water, then pack the bearings with grease beforehand and afterwards.

Launching trolley

Many road trailers incorporate a launching trolley, but if yours does not, it is worth getting one. A launching trolley is much lighter and easier to handle than a road trailer, and it can be run into the water without affecting the bearings. As with a trailer, make sure the boat fits snugly on the trolley and that there are no point loads. Choose wheels to suit the conditions in which you expect to launch; for sandy beaches, wide wheels will not tend to dig in as much as narrow ones.

Regulations

There are many regulations affecting the car-topping and trailing of boats, and the remarks that follow are for guidance only. It is up to you to find out what regulations apply to you, and to obey them. You should also remember that regulations may change from time to time, and that they vary from country to country. The following notes apply to the United Kingdom.

Car-topping

The carriage of a boat on the roof of a car is covered by the laws relating to dangerous loads. It is an offence to carry a load which might be a danger to the occupants of the car or anyone else. Overloading, excessive top weight and an insecure load would all be included in this. Anything that falls off the car into the road is clearly insecure, and can lead to prosecution.

Projecting loads

Anything which projects more than 3 ft (1 m) behind the car (or trailer) must be marked with a brightly coloured rag or something similar. If it projects more than 6 ft (1·8 m), it must be marked with a special triangular sign.

Lights

If a loaded trailer obscures the stop lights and the turn indicators of the towing car, then these lights must be repeated on the trailer. At night, a trailer must also carry two red lights to the rear and a white light to illuminate the number plate.

Brakes

Trailers of less than 2 cwt (100 kg) unladen weight need not be fitted with brakes. However if brakes are fitted, whether required by law or not, then they must be properly maintained.

Suspension

All road trailers must have an efficient form of springing or suspension to isolate the chassis from the road wheels.

Wings

Trailer wheels must be fitted with suitable wings (mudguards).

Tyres

The same regulations apply to trailer tyres as to car tyres; they must have adequate tread, be free of cuts and other damage, and be properly inflated. The penalty for a defective tyre on a trailer is the same as for one on a car.

Signs

A trailer should carry a reflective number plate with the same registration number as the towing car. It should also carry two standard reflective triangles of a specified size. For saloon and estate cars with seats for 8 people or less, these signs are not compulsory; but if they are not carried, then the trailer must be fitted with two red reflectors to the rear at night.

Speed limits

The following remarks apply to a trailer of less than 2 cwt (100 kg) unladen weight of the single axle type, not fitted with brakes. If such a trailer is towed by a private vehicle not exceeding 30 cwt (1·5 tonnes) unladen weight, then it may travel at 50 m.p.h. (provided no lower restriction is in force), subject to the following conditions:

1 The weight of the trailer and its load must not exceed 60 per cent of the kerbside weight of the towing vehicle.
2. The kerbside weight of the towing vehicle must be clearly marked, either inside or on the nearside externally.
3 The trailer, if a caravan or a trailer carrying fixed equipment, must be marked with its maximum gross weight on the nearside externally (this condition would not apply to a boat on a trailer, which is not 'fixed equipment').
4 The trailer must carry a plate with the number '50' facing to the rear. The dimensions of the plate and numbers are specified, but any plate bought for the purpose would almost certainly fit the regulations.

The *kerbside weight* of a vehicle is its weight without passengers or any load apart from fuel, water and normal tools, and the weight of the towing bracket.

The *maximum gross weight* of a trailer is the maximum weight of the trailer and the load for which it is designed to be used.

Weights may be expressed in kilograms or imperial measure, but the same units must be used for both car and trailer.

If you cannot comply with any of these conditions, then your speed is limited to 40 m.p.h. on all-purpose roads and motorways.

Dangerous loads

As with car-topping, the laws about dangerous loads apply. A common problem is a projecting outboard motor. This should be unshipped while trailing if at all possible; otherwise the propeller blades must be well padded.

Driving licence

A person with a provisional licence is not allowed to tow a trailer.

Insurance

As a final point, do check with your insurance company that your policy covers you for towing or for carrying a boat on the roof of the car. Neglect of this simple precaution could be both expensive and difficult.

9 Basic Seamanship

Seamanship is the art of handling your boat and its gear in a safe, efficient and easy way. In this chapter you will find some useful knots, a description of rigging the Ideal for sailing, and remarks on rowing and outboard motoring. The actual sailing of the boat (which is, of course, seamanship) is deferred to Chapter 10.

Knots

The knots used by seamen (which they usually call 'bends' or 'hitches') have been around for centuries, each one designed for its own specific purpose. The ideal knot is easy to tie and untie, never slips or jams, and does its job efficiently. The dinghy sailor only needs to know a few knots, but he should know them properly; a knot that comes undone or that jams can be dangerous as well as embarrassing.

The figure-eight knot (Figure 17)

This is one of the easiest knots to tie, and is used to form a stopper at the end of a rope. Its most common application is to prevent the loose end of a sheet from pulling through a block or fairlead, and you should put a figure-eight knot in the ends of your sheets as a matter of habit.

Round turn and two half hitches (Figure 18)

This knot is used to make the painter of a boat fast to a post. The rope is led round the post in a complete turn, and brought back; then two half hitches are tied in the standing part (the part attached to the boat). The knot can also be used to make a boat's painter fast to a ring, but the bowline is better for this job.

Bowline (Figure 19)

A superb knot for making a loop in a rope, and one of the most useful knots ever invented. Use it for making a rope fast to a ring, for joining two ropes together (by tying interlocking bowlines in each), or for any other purpose that occurs to you. It is pronounced 'bow-lin'.

Clove hitch (Figure 20)

A useful knot for making a light load fast to a post or similar object. It consists simply of two half hitches, tied one after the other. It can be made in the hand and dropped over the end of a short post.

The sheet bend (Figure 21)

This knot is used to join a rope to a loop (or bight) in the end of another rope. It is not particularly secure where the ropes may go slack and then jerk tight again; but for a steady load the sheet bend is excellent and the double sheet bend is even better. Sailors used the sheet bend to hold their hammocks up, so it must be reliable!

Rolling hitch (Figure 22)

This is also known as the stopper hitch. Its great merit is that it resists slipping along the rope on which it is tied. Its main use is to take the strain temporarily off another rope, so that the other rope can be adjusted in some way. It is also useful for lashing a cover down. Tie a rolling hitch as tightly as you can, or it will not work properly.

Reef knot (Figure 23)

Though very well known, the reef knot is not a particularly useful knot, except in its original job of tying down the reef points in a sail, where it is neat, unobtrusive and will not jam.

Securing to a cleat

A cleat is a fitting to which ropes can be made fast, and there are basically two types – jamming and non-jamming. To make fast to a

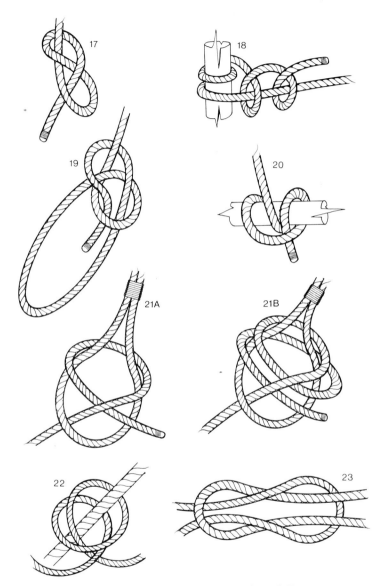

Figure 17: Figure-eight knot.

Figure 18: Round turn and two
half hitches.

Figure 19: Bowline.

Figure 20: Clove hitch.

Figure 21: (a) Sheet bend.
        (b) Double sheet bend.

Figure 22: Rolling hitch.

Figure 23: Reef knot.

jamming cleat, you merely jam the rope in, as you might expect. Remember that the rope might come out again if it goes slack, and that it is not difficult to trip a rope out of a jam cleat by accident. To make up a rope on a non-jamming cleat, start with a round turn around the body of the cleat, then make figures-of-eight around the horns; finish off with a round turn around the body of the cleat.

Rope ends

If any rope is cut, the ends will begin to fray unless they are protected. The ends of synthetic ropes can be sealed by melting the fibres together with a flame or hot blade. Ropes made from natural fibres should be whipped; a suitable whipping is shown in *Figure 24*. Chandlers now sell special sleeving which will stop fraying in the ends of both natural and synthetic ropes. The sleeving, which must be the right size for the rope, is slipped over the end and heated. It then shrinks to grip the rope's end tightly.

Figure 24: Common whipping. (*a*) First bury the end. (*b*) Then wind around a loop and pull tight. The length of the whipping should equal the diameter of the rope.

Rigging the Ideal for sailing

Before you leave home, make sure that you have everything that you will need, as nothing is more infuriating than to arrive at the water's edge and find you have left some vital part behind. For your first few excursions, it is a good idea to rig the boat completely before setting off. You will then be able to check all the gear, as well as gaining valuable practice in rigging the boat. Naturally, you will have to unrig the boat again before loading it on the car, but you will soon find that rigging and unrigging takes only a few minutes when you are used to it.

The mast

First, park the boat with its head into the wind, in a place where you have room to move around it. Then put the shrouds and the fore-stay on the masthead. The shrouds are two wires with a loop formed in one end and a shackle fitted at the other. The loops are pushed over the plastic moulding at the masthead, so that the shrouds lead down to port and starboard of the mast. The forestay is a similar wire, but is fitted with a lanyard (a short length of rope) at the bottom end. The loop is pushed over the masthead above the two shrouds, so as to lead down the forward side of the mast; you can tell which side of the mast is which by remembering that all the fittings on the bottom of the mast are on the after side. Fit the flag or burgee to the top of the mast, if that is where you like to have it, and then step the mast. The heel, or bottom of the mast, is led through the round hole in the foredeck, and the square heel fitting is seated firmly into the mast step on top of the centre buoyancy tank. Because of the various fittings at the base of the mast, it will only go through the hole in the foredeck in the correct way. Now, shackle the two shrouds to their chainplates at the sides of the boat; take the lanyard on the end of the forestay around the forward pin in the stem fitting, then lead it up and through the eye in the end of the forestay and bring it down again. Pull the lanyard hard, to make the shrouds and forestay really tight, and then fasten it off with a clove hitch.

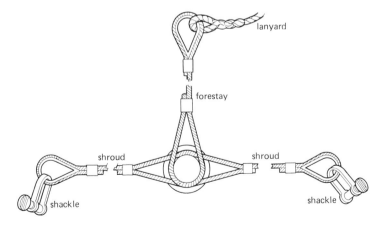

Figure 25: The arrangement of shrouds and forestay at the masthead.

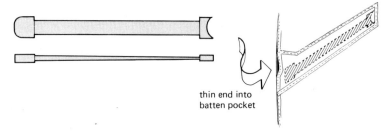

thin end into
batten pocket

Figure 26: A sail batten. The thin end goes into the batten pocket first.

The mainsail

Along the leech of the mainsail are three long pockets for the mainsail battens, which hold the leech of the sail in shape and make it
set better. The battens (shortest at the top) should be pushed into
the pockets and lodged firmly in position. The battens are thinner
at one end than the other; it is the thin end that should be pushed
into the pocket first. The mainsail can now be fitted to the gaff, by
feeding the roped luff of the sail through the groove in the gaff; start
with the head of the sail at the bottom end of the gaff, and pull it
up to the top (the peak). Shackle the head of the mainsail into
position, and fit the flag or burgee if you prefer to carry it at the peak
of the gaff.

Carry the gaff and mainsail to the boat, shackle the main halyard
to the lower of the two fittings on the gaff, and hoist the sail all the
way up. A short length of elastic cord is clipped around the mast at
the throat, to prevent the bottom of the gaff falling away from the
mast.

Fit the boom to the gooseneck on the mast, and make fast the
lanyard at the tack of the mainsail to the eye at the forward end
of the boom. Pull it tight, to make the luff of the sail taut, or the
boat will not perform as well as she should. Pass the lacing on the
luff of the mainsail round the mast and through the eyes in the sail

peak

halyard point for
reefed sail

normal halyard
fitting

throat

Figure 27: The gaff, showing the two halyard positions. The one near the
throat is for the normal mainsail; the one nearer the peak is for
the reefed mainsail.

between the throat and the tack, but do not make it too tight. The clew of the sail can now be made fast to the other end of the boom; again, this lashing should not be too tight. Pull it in until a diagonal crease just begins to appear in the sail.

Fit the main sheet to the boom end and to the rope horse which runs across the stern near the transom. The fall of the sheet, or the part that you hold, should come out at the bottom. Pull the sheet in tight, and fit the kicking strap between the boom and the foot of the mast. Pull the kicking strap tight and make it fast, then ease off the main sheet. The mainsail is now rigged and can be lowered into the boat, ready for re-hoisting after the boat has been launched.

The jib

The jib is, by comparison, a very easy sail to bend on. The middle of the jib sheet is first made fast to the clew of the sail, so that the sheet has two falls, one for each side of the boat. The tack of the sail is made fast to the after pin in the stemhead fitting, and the plastic hanks along the luff of the jib are clipped to the forestay. The fore halyard is bent on to the head of the sail, and the jib is ready for hoisting. The two sheet ends are led through their respective fairleads, and a figure-eight knot tied in the ends to stop them coming out again. When the jib is hoisted, it is essential that the luff of the sail should be really taut, as the sail will not set properly otherwise.

Apart from tidying up, only two things remain to be done. The centreboard should be fitted into its slot (but not lowered, of course), and the rudder should be shipped with the blade lifted up. Before you lower the sails, the boat should look like *Figure 3*.

Reefing

In strong winds, the sail area of the Ideal may be more than the crew can comfortably or safely deal with. In such conditions, the beginner is best advised to stay on shore, but the more experienced sailor can carry on by reefing, or reducing the area of the mainsail.

About two feet above the foot of the mainsail is a row of short rope pendants, called reef points. At the same height, there are strong cringles, or eyelets, worked into the luff and leech of the sail. To reef the mainsail, it must be lowered and re-hoisted, using the upper of the two fittings on the gaff. The sail is then re-set, using the cringles by the reef points in the luff and leech, instead of those at the tack and clew. Finally, the loose panel of sail which is no longer being used is bundled up neatly and secured with the reef points.

Rowing

There is little to be said about rowing a dinghy, as it is pretty straightforward and almost anyone can make some attempt to row a boat. However, there are a few tips which can make the process easier and more successful. First, make sure that the rowlocks are shipped properly, and are secured to the boat by a short piece of line; rowing becomes more than a little difficult if one of the rowlocks has been dropped over the side. Use short strokes, and keep the blades of the oars vertical all the time. Expert oarsmen 'feather' their oars on the return stroke, by turning the blades horizontal. Try this by all means, but do not be surprised if you 'catch a crab'. This happens when the oar goes into the water at an angle; either it skids across the water, making you fall over backwards into the bottom of the boat, or else the oar blade plunges deep into the water, bringing the boat to a dead stop.

When rowing along, you face towards the stern so it is not easy to see where you are going. Line up the boat in the direction you want to go, and then look astern to pick out some mark on the shore to steer by. Check that you have not gone off course by glancing over your shoulder every few moments. Like many boats not designed exclusively for rowing, the Ideal tends to round up into the wind, so that in a breeze you may find that you need to pull more strongly on one oar than the other to keep the boat going in a straight line.

Finally, the rowing position in the Ideal involves sitting across the centre buoyancy tank, right over the centreboard slot. As you row along, water tends to splash up this slot, so you should block it up or you will get a wet bottom. A short length of rubber hose is ideal (*Figure 28*).

Outboard motoring

The Ideal dinghy is designed for use with an outboard motor of between $1\frac{1}{2}$ and 5 horsepower. The motor should be fixed to the

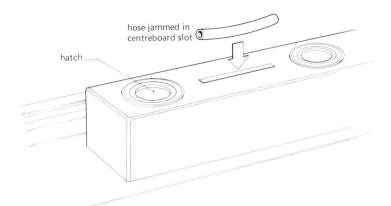

Figure 28: Jam a hose in the centreboard slot while rowing or under power, to prevent water splashing up.

transom fairly close to the centre line, on whichever side you prefer. I like to have the motor mounted to starboard, so that I can steer with my right hand. Make sure that the motor securing clamps are nicely tight, and tie the motor to the boat with some line as well, just in case the clamps work loose.

If you are alone in the boat, the bow tends to cock up in the air because your weight and the weight of the motor are concentrated in the stern. Correct this tendency as much as possible, by carrying ballast or cargo well forward, or by fitting an extension to the outboard's tiller so that you can sit further forward yourself. The boat can be difficult to manage if trimmed too much by the stern, and it is hard to see where you are going.

If you look after your outboard carefully, as described in the maker's handbook, it should give you years of trouble-free service. Always carry a few essential tools and spares in the boat with you, including a spare spark plug and plug spanner, and a spare shear pin and the tools to fit it. The shear pin protects the propeller and

Figure 29: (a) The boat should not be trimmed too much by the stern when outboarding. (b) A tiller extension on the outboard allows the helmsman to sit further forward, improving the trim.

engine if you hit something hard on the bottom. If the shear pin goes, you will want to change it on the water, so make sure that you have everything you need. You should also carry a pair of oars in case the motor fails and you cannot get it started again.

As when rowing, water tends to splash up the centreboard case when going along under outboard motor. A short length of rubber hose jammed into the slot will keep the water out of the boat.

10 Basic Sailing

Many people are under the impression that it is difficult to sail a boat, but in reality it is very easy. It takes a great deal of skill to extract the ultimate in performance from a sailing dinghy, but pottering about is literally child's play. Learning to sail is rather like learning to ride a bicycle; it seems hard at first, but as you learn it gets easier and easier, until you cannot imagine how you ever found it difficult in the first place. Learning to sail is like learning to ride a bicycle in another way, too. You cannot do either from a book; this chapter can only give you the basic principles of sailing, and advise you how to start. You will only learn to sail in a boat on the water.

To begin with, let us imagine that you and your boat have been miraculously transported into open water. The centreboard and rudder are down and a gentle wind is blowing over the starboard beam of the boat. You are sitting with your back to the wind, and the sail is flapping with the sheet eased right out. To make things simple, we will imagine that only the mainsail is set. Now pull in slowly on the main sheet, which is attached to the clew of the sail. Gradually the sail will stop flapping and fill with wind, and the boat will gather way. Keep on pulling in the main sheet until the sail is not flapping or lifting anywhere; when it has 'gone to sleep', as sailors put it. By now, the rudder will have started working, and you will be able to sail the boat along in a straight line. While all this was going on, the boat would have begun to heel and almost instinctively you would have moved yourself to the high side (to weather) to keep it upright (*Figure 30*). Now, ease out the mainsheet. The mainsail will start flapping again, the boat will slow down and it will stop trying to heel. Eventually the boat will stop and you will be back in the same situation from which you started.

The first thing to remember is that the sail not only makes the boat go along; it makes the boat heel as well. Both these things are

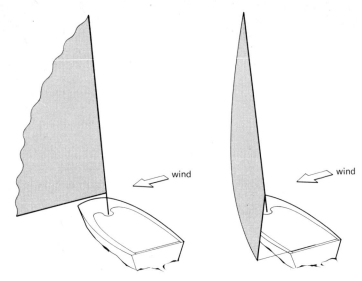

Figure 30: (*a*) The starting position. The wind is on the beam and the mainsail is flapping. (*b*) When the sheet is hardened in, the sail sets and the boat begins to move.

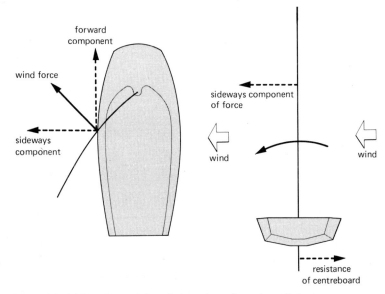

Figure 31: (*a*) The force of the wind on the sail can be split into two components. (*b*) The sideways component is resisted by the centreboard, causing the boat to heel.

controlled by the sheet, which is in a sense like the accelerator of a car; it controls the power you have available. Without going too deeply into theory, the flow of wind over the curved surface of the sail causes a force, which acts more or less at right angles to the sail (*Figure 31*). Part of this force acts along the fore-and-aft line of the boat, making it go along. Another part of the force tends to push the boat sideways. But the centreboard stops the boat going sideways, so it heels over instead.

So far, you have learned to sail along with the wind on the beam (beam reaching). Now turn the boat a few degrees towards the direction from which the wind is coming, by pushing the tiller away from you, towards the side on which the boom is. As the boat is heeled, it is not hard to see why this is called 'putting the tiller down'. When the boat turns towards the direction of the wind, it is said to luff. The front edge of the sail (the luff) will start to lift and the boat will lose power; it will slow down and not heel so much. Now pull in on the sheet until the sail goes to sleep again. Power will be restored, the boat will gather speed again and begin to heel – rather more strongly than before, so you may have to move a bit further up to weather to balance her. You can repeat this luffing process, each time sailing a little closer to the wind, until the boom is almost fore-and-aft. You cannot pull the sheet in any more, and if you luff even further the sail will start to lift and you will not be able to do anything about it. This limiting position, with the boom pulled right in and the boat sailing as close to the wind as she will go, is called sailing close hauled (*Figure 32*). You will find that the wind is about 45° on the starboard bow, so it is now possible to understand how a boat can sail against the wind. She will not go directly into the wind, as you have discovered, but she will go at 45° or so to the wind. By following a zig-zag course, with the wind first on one bow and then on the other, you can make progress to windward. This process is called beating, or working to windward.

So far, the wind in our example has been blowing over the starboard side of the boat, with the boom to port. The boat is said to be on the starboard tack; if you are trying to beat to windward, there will come a time when you want to put the wind on the other bow, so that the boat is on the port tack. The boat must be turned through the eye of the wind until the sail fills again on the other side. This is called tacking (*Figure 33*).

Tacking is very straightforward, but must be done smartly. As

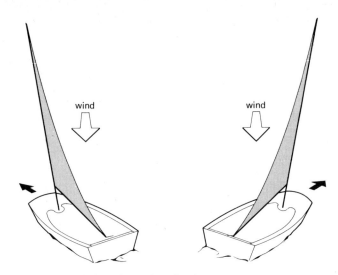

Figure 32: Closehauled on the starboard tack.
Figure 33: Closehauled on the port tack.

the boat comes head to wind you lose all the drive from the sail; if you are slow in tacking the boat can lose headway, the rudder will stop working and you will lie stopped head to wind, or 'in irons'. Eventually, the boat will gather sternway and pay off on one tack or the other, but you may not be able to choose which. There is nothing dangerous about getting in irons, but it is irritating and unseamanlike, though when beating in very light airs it sometimes cannot be helped.

You have decided to tack. 'Ready about,' you say firmly to yourself (when you have a crew, he will need to know). Push the tiller firmly down to leeward, duck under the boom as the boat comes head to wind (*mind your head*), change over the hands holding the mainsheet and the tiller, and then stop the boat swinging as soon as the sail fills on the new tack. Easy, isn't it? Settle yourself down, make sure that you are sailing properly close hauled on the new tack, and sort out the jumble that the mainsheet will have got itself into. Now you are all ready to tack again, so keep on doing it until it becomes second nature.

However, there will come a moment when you either run out of water or get further from home than you care to go, and you will want to come back again. You have to bear away, which is the exact

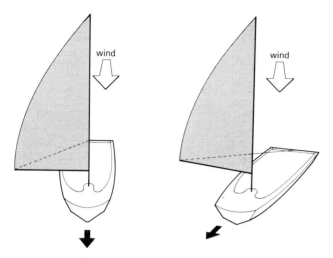

Figure 34: Running.
Figure 35: Running by the lee.

opposite of luffing up; put the tiller gently up (towards you), and at the same time ease out the sheet. Easing the sheet is important; if you do not, the heeling force will quickly get bigger and could capsize you if you did nothing about it. As you gradually bear away, the boom goes further out and you will soon be back in the beam-reaching position from which you started. But you can go on bearing away, easing the sheet all the time, until the wind is right astern and the boom is at right angles to the boat. You are now running and on this point of sailing you can no longer control the speed of the boat with the sheet, because it is eased out as far as it will go. If you want to slow down, you have to luff up to spill the wind from the sail (*Figure 34*).

Now comes a manoeuvre which can be dangerous to anyone who doesn't know exactly what he is doing. If you continue to turn in the same direction, the stern of the boat will pass through the eye of the wind and you will be running by the lee (*Figure 35*). The danger arises if the wind gets behind the mainsail and slams it violently from one side to the other. This can cause damage to the boat, injury to anyone unlucky enough to connect with the swinging boom, and it can also cause a capsize. The involuntary gybe, as this unpleasant event is called, is to be avoided at all costs. But a controlled gybe is a perfectly seamanlike thing to do, though it should be approached with care. It is rather like turning a car across a stream of traffic – dangerous if you do not know what you are doing, but perfectly safe otherwise.

To gybe in a controlled way, sail with the wind on the quarter and harden the sheet until the sail is fairly well in (in very light winds, hardening the sheets is not really necessary). Turn the boat firmly and steadily until the boom swings over your head. The shortened main sheet will limit its travel, and hence the force with which it swings. IMMEDIATELY ease the sheet until the sail is set as it was before, on the other tack. As there is little or no heeling force when running, you will probably start the gybe sitting more or less on the centre line, but be ready to move out on the new weather side if your timing is a bit astray and the boat tries to heel at the moment of gybing. When you have a crew, he can help a gybe by swinging the boom across with his hand as the stern passes through the wind. This makes the gybe less violent. When running, and especially when gybing, the centreboard should be only about half way down. The boat sails better and, when gybing, there is less chance of the boat 'stumbling' over its own centreboard which may lead to a capsize.

Gybing is not recommended in strong winds, when even a controlled gybe may be chancy. Reefing the main would help but in a boat with a jib you may do well enough downwind (and certainly be safer) with the mainsail down, running under jib alone. Treat gybing with caution until you have gained some experience; do not be ashamed to go right round in a circle, tacking instead of gybing, if you have any doubts at all.

The jib

So far we have been sailing our boat with only the mainsail, but most dinghies (including the Ideal) normally set a smaller sail called the jib, forward of the mast. The jib works in exactly the same way as the mainsail; the only significant difference is that the jib has two sheets, one on each side, whereas the mainsail has one sheet that slides across as you change tack. Setting a jib makes sailing the boat a bit more complicated for two reasons; first, the two sails interact with each other so that it takes practice to get them working together properly, and secondly, you will normally have a crew with you to look after the jib sheet. You and your crew must work together to get the best out of the boat.

To get a reasonable set for a mainsail and jib, begin by setting the main on its own, with the jib sheets eased. Then harden the jib sheets until the luff of the jib stops lifting. At this point, you will probably find that the luff of the mainsail is lifting because of the interaction with the jib, so harden the main sheet until the sail is set properly. Finally, trim the jib sheet so that the jib is just asleep. The two sails will now be working together, and you will be surprised to see what difference the fairly small jib can make to the speed of the boat.

When sailing close hauled, the main and jib sheets have both been hardened right in; to make the best progress to windward, you must now steer the boat so as to keep the sails properly filled. If you sail too close to the wind, the luff of the jib will start to lift, the boat will lose speed and you are said to be 'pinching'. If you bear away from the close-hauled point of sailing, the boat will speed up and heel more; but you will not be sailing as close to the wind as is possible, so you will make less progress to windward. The technique of sailing close hauled is to luff up gently until the jib starts to lift, and then bear away until it goes to sleep again. Do this every minute or so and you will not be caught out by unexpected wind shifts. The key point to remember is that when you are close hauled, the wind dictates your course; as the wind changes direction, so must you.

When to tack

Because you cannot sail directly towards an objective which is to windward, you have to decide which tack to start on and when to tack. For a mark close at hand, the simplest tactic is to start off on the making tack, that is the one which takes you closer to your objective; go on the other tack when the objective is abeam, and you will finish up fairly close to it, though you may have to put in another short tack as you approach. If you have a longish beat in front of you, then start off on the making tack as before. Stay on this tack until the objective is dead to windward, then work up towards it in a series of short tacks. By doing this, you put yourself in a position where any wind shift that comes along works to your advantage (*Figure 36*).

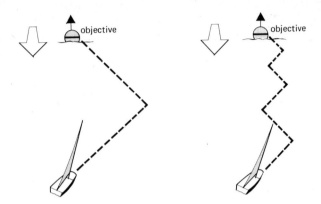

Figure 36: Tacking tactics. (a) If the object is close, start on the making track and go about when the object is abeam. (b) For a distant mark, make short tacks up the line of the wind.

Tacking with two

When you have a crew on board, you must let him know what you intend to do, so that he can work properly with you. When you decide to tack, say, 'Ready about', to warn him. When you are both ready, say, 'Lee-oh', and put the tiller down. As the boat comes up into the wind, the crew lets the old jib sheet fly, he ducks under the boom as it swings over and then he hardens the new jib sheet as the boat settles on the other tack.

Running and gybing with a jib

On a run, you will probably find that the jib collapses, because it is blanketed by the mainsail. To get the jib working again, you can get your crew to try setting it on the other side of the mast so that you are sailing goose winged *(Figure 37)*. When you want to gybe, warn the crew by saying, 'Stand by to gybe.' He should make sure that the centreboard is half way up. When both of you are ready, say, 'Gybe-oh,' and gybe the boat exactly as before. As the boat comes stern to wind, the crew should grab the boom and help it across over his head. When on the new tack, he can get the jib set in his own time.

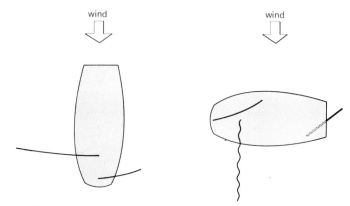

Figure 37: Running goosewinged.
Figure 38: Heaving to. The gib is set aback, the main is flapping and the helm is to leeward.

Heaving to

After all these exhausting manoeuvres you may feel like stopping the boat for a bit of a rest or to think about what you would like to do next. You could anchor, but this would be a lot of work for a few minutes pause; or you could let go of the sheets and the tiller and leave the boat to her own devices. A more tidy way to keep the boat more or less stopped is to heave to. This is done by backing the jib, or sheeting it on the weather side of the boat, using the weather sheet (*Figure 38*); ease the main sheet so that the mainsail is no longer drawing; and put the tiller down to leeward. Now the wind is trying to turn the boat one way by blowing on the backed jib, and the rudder is trying to turn the boat the other way. The result is a balance, with the boat lying quietly more or less beam on to the wind. Boats vary in their ability to heave to, and you may need to take in on the mainsheet slightly to get the balance exact.

Man (or anything else) overboard

It is not particularly often that anyone falls out of a dinghy, but it is as well to know what to do just in case. It is rather more likely that some vital possession like a hat, a thermos flask or a teddy bear gets dropped over the side. Provided the object floats, it is best for family relations to get it back again.

There is only one difference between picking up a man and picking up a teddy bear; until he went over the side, the man was your crew, and you are now single-handed. Forget about the jib, just cast off the sheet, and sail the boat under main alone. Now treat your errant crew as if he were a teddy bear; he has his personal buoyancy and unless he has been injured (possible but unlikely), he is in no danger. One very good reason, incidentally, for making sure your crew can handle the tiller as well as you can, is the possibility that *you* might go over the side and your crew has to come back for you.

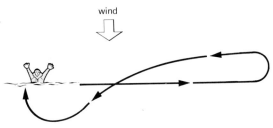

Figure 39: Picking up a man overboard.

Assume for the moment that the ship's company is present and correct, except for a teddy bear which is fast disappearing astern. The simplest procedure, whatever point of sailing you are on, is to alter course to put the wind on the beam and reach away from the object. As soon as you are ready, but without hurrying, tack and reach back again towards the object. Point the boat a little to leeward of the object and as you approach, let the jib sheet fly. Then progressively ease the mainsheet, which will slow the boat down. As you reach the object, luff up hard to spill the wind from the mainsail and stop the boat. If your judgement has been correct, the object should be within easy reach (*Figure 39*).

Picking up a buoy

If there is no current, you can treat a buoy exactly as if it were a floating object like a teddy bear. But if a tide or current is running it is essential to approach the buoy by stemming the flow of water. If the wind is against the tide, drop the mainsail and approach under jib alone, spilling the wind from it as necessary to control your speed (*Figure 40a*). If the wind is across the tide, reach towards the

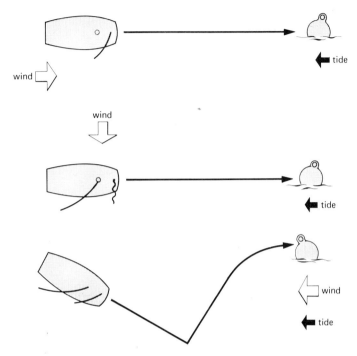

Figure 40: Picking up a buoy: (*a*) wind against tide; (*b*) wind across tide; (*c*) wind and tide together.

buoy while stemming the tide, and control your speed with the sheets (*Figure 40b*). It is only when the wind and tide are in the same direction that nice judgement is called for. Beat up to the buoy, and so judge your final tack that you can luff up head to wind and tide, lose way and stop over the buoy. If you get it wrong (as you probably will), do not leave your crew hanging desperately onto the buoy as you shoot past at high speed – tell him to let go, then go round and try again (*Figure 40c*).

Coming alongside

When coming alongside a jetty or pontoon, the essential thing is again to stem the current if one is flowing. If there is no current, then come alongside, as near as possible head to wind. Aim to bring the boat to rest a few inches away from the jetty, within easy grabbing distance (*Figure 41*).

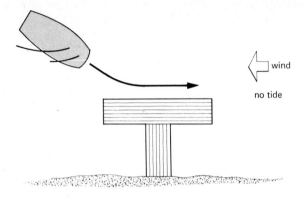

Figure 41: Coming alongside (no tide).

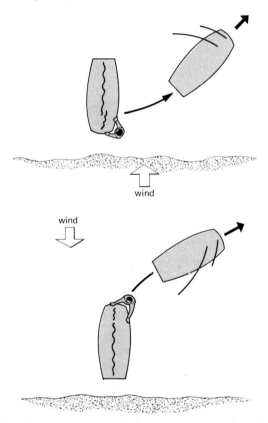

Figure 42: Leaving a beach: (*a*) weather shore; (*b*) Lee shore.

Leaving a beach

If you launch your boat from a beach, it's a simple matter to get away if the wind is blowing off the shore (a weather shore), or if the wind is blowing along the line of the beach. You will have rigged and launched the boat and your crew will be standing in the water holding her head to wind (unless you both wear boots, wet feet are inevitable). When everything is ready, the crew pushes the bow to seaward and climbs in. You may need to back the jib to push the boat's head round. Then harden in the sheets and sail off, not forgetting to put the rudder and centreboard down as the water deepens (*Figure 42a*).

With the wind blowing on to the shore (a lee shore), things are a little more difficult. The crew will be holding the boat head to wind as before, but he will be standing in deeper water. When you are ready, decide which tack is the better for making an offing, back the jib appropriately, get the crew aboard and sail off close hauled. Get way on the boat and get the centreboard down as soon as possible, or you may be blown back ashore. If this does happen, your long-suffering crew has to hop over the side again to hold the boat ready for another try (*Figure 42b*).

Coming in to a beach

This is a much simpler operation than sailing off a beach; on a weather shore, or with the wind parallel to the beach, reach or sail close hauled to your objective and take off speed by easing sheets as you approach. Do not forget to pull up the rudder and centre-board as the water shallows, or you may be forcibly reminded of your neglect when the boat grounds in waist-deep water. On a lee shore, round up head to wind some way off shore and drop the mainsail; then run in under jib alone. In all cases, the crew should hop over the side just before the boat grounds and steady the boat, holding her head to wind until you have got the sail off her.

Sailing in crowded waters

Many sailing areas are full of moored boats, boats under sail and power and sometimes people swimming. Keep a good lookout all the time and obey the sailor's rule of the road (Chapter 11). Even a small dinghy can injure a swimmer, so keep well clear of them. Watch out for the blind spot behind a low-cut jib (some jibs have a transparent window). Dinghies lying to moorings often have a long painter in the water between them and the buoy. If you sail gaily across this painter, you may find your rudder or centreboard hooked up in an embarrassing way. Equally, launching ramps and hards often extend under water for some distance. If you cut too close to the end, you may hit the rigid structure with your centreboard; at best this will give you a nasty shock, and at worst it might damage the centreboard case.

Capsizing

Dinghies are not intended to capsize and if you are careful and alert there is no reason why you ever should. Racing dinghies capsize more often than cruising dinghies because their crews are trying to push the boat to the limit and it is easy to try just a little bit too hard. The cruising man, with only safety and enjoyment on his mind, should never need to press his boat to the extent that a capsize is likely. Still, anything can happen, and every skipper and crew should know what to do if the unlikely takes place. It then becomes an unplanned ducking, rather than a dangerous situation.

Capsizes generally take place surprisingly slowly – almost majestically. It is often possible to avert a capsize, even at a late stage, by letting go of everything – sheets and tiller – so that the boat loses all drive and all heeling force, and flies up into the wind.

There are various ways of righting a dinghy after a capsize, but they have much in common. The basic principles are:

1   Keep in contact with the boat at all times.
2   Let off the mainsheet, so the boat will not sail away from you when she is righted.
3   Make sure the centreboard is down.
4   Pull down on the centreboard to right the boat, or stand on it, using the jib sheet to steady yourself.
5   Clamber aboard and bail out the water. It is at this moment that you will be glad that you made all loose gear fast to the boat before you set off.
6   The crew can either hang on to the boat, holding her steady, or can tuck himself into the hull, so that he gets scooped up as the helmsman gets the boat upright.

11 Sense and Safety

The whole point of going on to the water is to enjoy yourself, but it is as well to remember that nature has constructed us to live on land. Afloat, we are moving into an alien and potentially hostile environment. As with all human activities, there are risks; but if you understand the risks and take sensible precautions to guard against them, you need never feel that you are taking yourself and your crew into danger.

This chapter may appear to be a rather daunting list of do's and don'ts. It is not intended as such, but rather as a checklist for the skipper. Accept or reject each item as you see fit, according to the circumstances. You need to be much better prepared if you are going out to sea, because the sea is so big. On a flooded gravel pit, a compass is just extra weight; at sea it is essential. The various items in this checklist have been grouped into three sections: personal gear, boat gear, and things to think about.

Personal gear

These things are the responsibility of each crew member, but the skipper should make sure that they have been brought.

Ability to swim

Every person in the boat *must* be able to swim; there should be no exceptions allowed in any circumstances. This leads to a problem with small children who have not yet learned to swim, and who will object loud and long to being left behind. It is best, though, to harden your heart even though a likely consequence is that someone else will have to stay behind as well to look after the child. You can console yourself with the thought that the child will be encouraged to learn to swim quickly, so he can join in the fun.

Personal buoyancy

Every crew member should have personal buoyancy of an approved type, and they should wear it all the time in the boat. There are two types to choose from. A standard life-jacket as supplied to sea-going ships is designed to support the wearer with his face above the water, even when unconscious. While very efficient, it is bulky and gets in the way in a small boat, and it prevents swimming almost entirely. A more suitable form of buoyancy for small boats is the buoyancy aid which gives less support but is much more convenient. The buoyant waistcoat type of aid is best, because it obstructs the wearer least.

Knife

Every sailor should carry a sharp knife, preferably with a spike as well.

Clothing

Clothing should be suited to the conditions, bearing in mind that it is always cooler on the water than you expect. Allow for the conditions changing; a baking hot calm at noon can very quickly turn into a cool, brisk Force 4 as the sea breeze comes in during the afternoon. You will need non-slip rubber-soled boots or shoes to keep your feet warm (and dry, if you are fussy); some sort of waterproof clothing to protect you from rain or spray; and a hat. If you wear spectacles or sunglasses, tie them round your head with a bit of light line, and keep something handy with which to wipe the lenses.

Boat gear

Buoyancy

The boat should have enough buoyancy to keep her well afloat under all circumstances. The drain plugs of built-in buoyancy tanks should fit properly and be in place; buoyancy bags should be firmly secured, fully inflated and properly plugged.

Baler

You need a baler to get water out of the boat. You can fit self-balers which suck out the water automatically, but as they only work when the boat is going along, you need the ordinary kind as well. Put a lanyard on it and make sure it is secured to the boat. A sponge is useful for mopping out the last few drops.

Oars or paddles

Carry them as an auxiliary way of getting back to shore if something goes wrong. Oars need rowlocks, so make sure they are in the boat as well, and are tied on.

Anchor and warp

When a boat is away from the shore, there is only one way to make it stay in one place, and that is to drop an anchor (if you heave to, the boat is still moving slowly, and is subject to tides and currents). The anchor warp (rope) should be about three times longer than the depth of water. Ten fathoms (20 metres) should be plenty. This warp can be used for towing as well.

Compass

In many sailing locations, a compass is quite unnecessary. At sea, however, and on large stretches of open water it is essential. Fog can sweep across suddenly and leave you totally lost. Even a small pocket compass is enough to tell you which way home lies.

Torch

If there is the faintest chance of being overtaken by darkness, you should take a torch with you, both to see what you are doing and to give warning of your presence to another boat.

Flares

If you wish to go some way out to sea, take some hand-held red flares in case you want to make a distress signal. Four is a good number of flares to carry. If you have to use them, let them off in pairs, rather than one at a time. You can also carry orange smoke signals for daytime use, but these are not particularly effective in strong winds.

Chart

If you do not know the area in which you are sailing, a chart will show you where to go and where not to go. Local knowledge is useful, too. Ask around and you will pick up all sorts of useful bits of information and meet some nice people into the bargain.

Spares

If you are using the outboard motor, take a reserve can of fuel, a funnel, a spare spark plug and a spare shear pin. You will also need the necessary tools to fit these items (Chapter 9).

Food

Some high-energy food such as chocolate or biscuits is useful in case you find yourself much later getting back than you expected. Take something to drink as well.

Things to think about

The weather

Any small boat is at the mercy of the weather, which can be very fickle. A sailing boat depends on the wind to make it go, but there is only a narrow range of wind speeds in which it is comfortable or prudent to cruise a dinghy. Be sure to get a weather forecast before you set out, and keep an eye open for changes in the sky which may warn of more wind to come. If you decide to reef, do it early rather than late because it is a much easier operation before the wind starts blowing hard. If you sail from the coast, you should be aware of the possibility of a sea breeze. This can start to blow on hot summer afternoons. It will set in at about one or two o'clock and freshen throughout the afternoon; it will begin to die away as the sun gets lower in the sky. A full-blooded sea breeze can reach

Plate 25: The Ideal with a reefed mainsail.

Force 4 or 5, so do not sail if such a breeze is likely unless you are ready for it. The sea breeze, as its name implies, blows from the sea to the land.

Tides

As everyone knows, the tide comes in and out at regular intervals on most coasts. This obviously causes the depth of water to change, so that at high water a dinghy may be able to sail over a sandbank which is exposed at low water. But this vertical movement of the water is accompanied by horizontal movements as the water flows to fill or empty bays or rivers. These horizontal movements are called tidal streams, and you need to understand something about them for several reasons:

1 You travel more quickly over the ground if the tidal stream is behind you rather than against you. But beware! It is only too easy to run off with the wind and tide behind you and make splendid progress in what feels like ideal conditions. Things will look very different when you turn back and have to beat home against a foul tide.
2 Generally, when the wind and the tide are in opposite directions (wind over tide), the sea is rougher than when they flow in the same direction.
3 Tidal streams flow very much more strongly around headlands than they do in bays.
4 Near headlands and in places where the sea bottom is irregular, the tidal streams can cause a violent sea to form, which can be dangerous for small craft. These areas of disturbed water are called 'overfalls' or 'races'. They are marked on the chart and should be avoided.

Local knowledge

It is never a good idea to take your boat and trusting crew to a strange place and just set off into the blue. Look at a chart and talk to the locals. Not only will they be able to warn you of unexpected pitfalls in the area; they may also tell you about delightful places to visit that you would never have found on your own. If sailing in an area where sand and mud banks abound, it is worth bearing

in mind that a tempting stretch of water empty of other boats is very
likely to be shallow.

Overloading

It is up to the skipper to decide how many people his boat can carry
in any particular circumstances. Do not overload your boat, as you
may live to regret it bitterly. Then again, you may not.

Information

Whenever you set off in your dinghy, there should be someone on
shore who knows your plans, so that they can raise the alarm if
anything should go wrong. If you are forced to change your plans,
by taking refuge from a sudden blow for example, then let your
contact ashore know about it; otherwise an expensive and unnecessary search-and-rescue operation may be started on your behalf.

Rule of the road

The mariner's highway code is ominously entitled 'The Collision
Regulations', and it applies to all vessels on the high seas or connec-
ted waterways. The authorities controlling inland waters often make
local byelaws with the same provisions. From a dinghy sailor's
point of view, the rules to remember are:

1   Steam does not give way to sail if the powered vessel is navigating
    along a narrow channel that you wish to cross. In general, keep
    clear of commercial traffic; a motor yacht ought to keep out
    of your way.
2   If two sailing vessels are likely to collide, then the one on the
    port tack has to give way to the one on the starboard tack
    (*Figure 43a*). If the two sailing vessels are on the same tack, then
    the boat to windward gives way to the boat to leeward (*Figure
    43b*).
3   Any overtaking vessels, under sail or power, must keep clear of
    the vessel being overtaken.
4   At night you must have a light available to indicate your position
    to another vessel; a torch is quite suitable. In fog, you need
    something to make a noise, like a whistle.

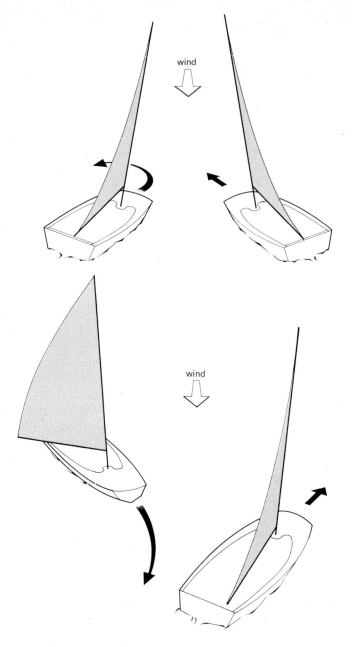

Figure 43: Rule of the road. (*a*) Boat A (on port tack) gives way to boat B. (*b*) Both A and B are on port tack, but A gives way as she is to windward of B.

5 By far the best plan is to keep out of everyone else's way; your dinghy draws very little water, so keep where it is shallow, out of the shipping channels and crowded areas.

Exposure

It can get bitterly cold at sea which leads to the risk of exposure, especially if you are wet into the bargain. Exposure, also known as hypothermia, is more common in fit young men than it is in women and older men; heat escapes more readily from their bodies. The early symptons of exposure are lethargy and immobility. The cure is to keep warm, keep dry and keep moving. Exposure can make itself felt even on a gravel pit; in spring and autumn the air and water temperatures can be very low indeed. Racing crews often wear wet suits to keep warm, but a wet suit is hardly appropriate for a family outing in a dinghy.

Capsizing

Capsizing is discussed in Chapter 10, but it is worth stressing the golden rule – whatever happens, stay with the boat. Incident after incident has proved that people who stay with their boat are generally rescued, while those who swim for the shore are often drowned. Better still, obey the even more golden rule – never capsize.

Distress signals

There are a number of internationally recognized distress signals. The ones that a dinghy sailor might come across are:

  Red flares
  Orange smoke signals
  Slowly and repeatedly raising and lowering outstretched arms.

Insurance

You should insure your boat, not only against accidental loss or damage to your boat, but also for Third Party risks. Take the advice of a broker who understands boat insurance.

12 Care of your Boat

Having invested money and effort in building a boat, you will want it to last, and so you will have to look after it. A modern dinghy like the Ideal is remarkably robust. The panels are made up of top-quality marine plywood; the joints of glass-fibre tape and resin are secure and strong, as are the glued joints; the design of the boat makes it strong and rigid; and over all is a carefully built-up protective coat of paint and varnish. With simple care and maintenance there is no reason why such a boat should not give many years of service.

As soon as possible after sailing, you should wash the boat down thoroughly, inside and out, with clean fresh water. Then dry it off well, paying particular attention to cracks and corners where water can lodge. The harder it is to reach a corner, the more important it is to do so, because it is in these inaccessible spots that the paint or varnish protection may break down unnoticed. Remove the plugs of the buoyancy tanks to drain and air them. If a lot of water comes out of a drain hole, then you clearly have a leak in the tank which should be repaired; a few drops of water are of no significance and should merely be mopped up. Leave the drain plugs out until you next want to use the boat.

Having washed and dried your boat, you should then inspect it carefully for damage. Minor scrapes and abrasions can let water into the fibres of the wood where it will eventually lead to rot. Sand around these areas, make sure that the wood is dry, and then touch up the paint or varnish. Check the sails, spars and other equipment before you put the boat away and repair or replace any damaged parts as soon as possible. Delay is fatal, as you are bound to forget until it is too late to do anything before you next want to go out.

When you put the boat away, do everything you can to keep it dry. Keep it under cover if at all possible, or else put a properly fitting boat cover over it. If neither of these is possible, store the boat upside down on some blocks to keep it off the ground. Do not let grass grow up around the boat as grass holds water which will break through your defences if left there for extended periods of time. Remember, too, that your boat is a large light structure, and it does not take much wind to blow it about. A good gale could easily leave it up a tree or in the neighbour's greenhouse, so make sure it is lashed down to something firm. Leaving the boat lashed to a road trailer would be all right for ordinary weather, but if it really started to blow you should peg the trailer itself down.

Refitting

At the end of the season your boat will still be looking quite respectable, provided you have looked after it, but the initial sparkle will have been rubbed off. The object of refitting is to put this sparkle back and even to improve it. Refitting is in no way a chore; it can offer as much pleasure as building and sailing the boat, and is an agreeable way of filling your leisure hours when the weather makes sailing unattractive.

The first step in refitting is to inspect the boat and all its gear minutely, making a list of everything that needs to be done and the materials that will have to be bought. Plan the order of the work, because some jobs may conflict with others. For example, it would be sensible to move a cleat or fairlead before repainting the boat so that the old screw holes could be made good before the new coat of paint is applied. Other jobs may take time – a sail sent to a sail-maker for repair may be away for weeks at busy times.

Here are some of the things to look for.

Sails

Check the stitching, especially where the wear is heavy near the clew and batten pockets. Look for wear and damage at the edges and the corners of the sails. Make sure that such things as the headboard, cringles and reef points are secure. Small stitching jobs on sails can easily be done at home, using a sailmaker's palm and needle, but damage of a more fundamental nature is best entrusted to a sail-maker.

Mast and spars

Examine them carefully for signs of wear and damage, and make sure all the fittings are secure. The most likely place for wear to show is in the halyard sheaves, especially the jib halyard. If the fitting has been correctly designed, the pin of the sheave will be made of softer material than the sheave itself, and will have taken most of the wear. The pin is quite easy to replace. Wooden spars will need to be rubbed down and re-varnished, while metal spars appreciate a coat of car polish.

Standing and running rigging

The standing rigging is the name given to the wires and fittings which hold the mast up. The stemhead fitting and the shroud chainplates should be checked to see that they are secure and in good condition. The shrouds and forestay should be inspected for broken strands, splices pulling out or crippling (kinking). If any of these is present, the wire should be replaced. Otherwise, stainless steel wires can be washed in fresh water, dried, rubbed with a light machine oil and put away. Galvanized steel wire rope should be rubbed with boiled linseed oil to protect it from rust.

The running rigging is the name given to all the ropes and wires used to control the sails and spars. Almost all ropes are now made from synthetic materials and are very strong and long-lived. All they need is a wash. Sheets and rope halyards should be turned end for end to equalize the wear. Wire halyards should be treated in the same way as the standing rigging, but damage is more likely because of the greater wear they get. Some halyards are made of wire with a rope tail; inspect the rope-to-wire splice carefully. Check the ends of all ropes to make sure they are not fraying. If they are, refer to Chapter 9 for remedial action.

Fittings

Make sure all fittings are still securely fastened, are not worn and are still working efficiently. Clean them up and lubricate moving parts where appropriate.

Centreboard and rudder

Check these particularly for damage to the leading edge, caused by hitting things while sailing. Any such damage should be made good, as it affects the boat's performance. They will then need a rub down and a coat of varnish. Check the gudgeons and pintles upon which the rudder is hinged, and the bolt on which a lifting rudder pivots. Also examine the device used to hold the centreboard down while sailing. This is often a piece of rubber cord, which tends to perish; replace it if necessary.

The hull

The hull should be thoroughly cleaned and dried and then inspected minutely. Any defects found should be repaired and any temporary repairs put in during the season should be made permanent. Move any fittings you want to move, and make good the holes. The boat is now ready for repainting. If the existing paint is sound and you wish to repaint it the same colour, then it is only necessary to make good any small defects, rub down with wet-or-dry (Chapter 7) and put on one or two coats of gloss top coat. If the colour is to be changed then you should rub down well and go through the full procedure described in Chapter 7, omitting only the priming and filling stages. Sound varnish can be rubbed down, and one or more new coats of varnish applied. If the varnish is in bad condition, you have to scrape it all off until you get back to bare wood and start again. Skarsten scrapers are very good for taking off varnish as they are easily sharpened and the blades can be changed when they wear out. It is essential that the scraper be razor-sharp. You will also need a combination shave-hook for awkward corners. If you need to remove paint, then a chemical stripper is probably easier to use than a blowtorch. The stripper should be properly 'killed' after it has done its work, as described on the container.

Repairs to plywood hulls

Plywood is remarkably tough and is generally only damaged by impact with something sharp – the bow of another boat, or an

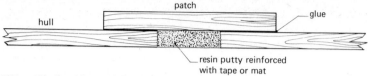

Figure 44: Patching a plywood hull.

anchor fluke sticking up from the bottom. The easiest way to repair a small crack is with a glass-fibre repair kit which contains a hard-setting, durable resin putty. The area of the crack should be scraped free of paint or varnish, any loose whiskers or flakes of ply removed with a sharp chisel and the resulting depression filled with resin

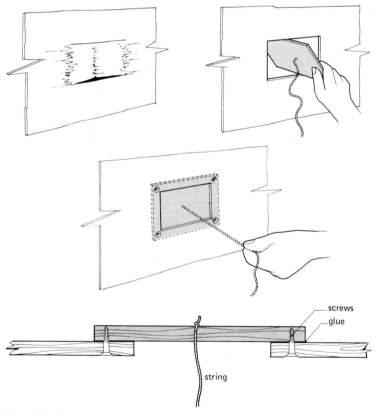

Figure 45: If the hole cannot be reached from inside the boat, use a piece of string to fit the patch in place, and hold it with screws while the glue sets.

putty. When the paste has hardened it can be sanded level with the surface and painted.

If the hole is too big for this technique, then you will have to put on a patch (*Figure 44*). Cut away the damaged wood and on the inside, mark a rectangle round the hole which overlaps it by at least ¾ in. (2 cm) all round. Remove the paint or varnish from this area, and glue on a plywood patch. Put the glue on the hull and the hardener on the patch. Wedge it firmly in position until the glue has set. The depression on the outside of the hull can now be filled with resin putty, reinforced with glass-fibre tape or mat. When hard, the resin putty can be sanded down and painted.

If the hole leads into a buoyancy tank, so that you cannot work on it from the inside of the boat, then you have to cut a rectangular hole around the damaged area (*Figure 45*). Then cut a plywood patch about two inches bigger all round than the hole. Drill a small hole in the middle of the patch and fix a length of string to it. Clean off the paint from the inside of the hole and apply glue. Put hardener on the patch and 'post' it through the hole; then twist it round and pull it back with the string until the patch covers the hole. Hold the patch in place with screws. The rectangular depression (which used to be a hole) can now be filled, either with resin putty or with a plywood patch cut to size.

If you are unlucky enough to suffer major damage to a frameless plywood dinghy, it can be difficult to repair. You should seek the advice of a professional boat-builder.

Index